CAN JUDAISM BE SAVED?
Its Future after Gaza

Arthur Green

Ben Yehuda Press
Teaneck, New Jersey

CAN JUDAISM BE SAVED? © **2025 Arthur Green**. All rights reserved. No part of this book may be used or reproduced in any manner whatsoever without written permission except in the case of brief quotations embodied in critical articles and reviews.

Published by Ben Yehuda Press
122 Ayers Court #1B
Teaneck, NJ 07666
BenYehudaPress.com

To subscribe to our monthly book club and support independent Jewish publishing, visit patreon.com/BenYehudaPress

Ben Yehuda Press books may be purchased at a discount by synagogues, book clubs, and other institutions buying in bulk. For information, please email markets@BenYehudaPress.com.

ISBN13 978-1-963475-84-5 paper 978-1-963475-85-2 epub

25 26 27 / 10 9 8 7 6 5 4 3 2 1   20251029

In Memory of all the innocent victims of this terrible conflict

And of my dear sister Paula Green
פערלא בת מרדכי ועטל

Contents

Prologue	vii
Preface	ix
Introduction	1
Our Biblical Legacy	12
Judaism and Christianity: The Parting of the Ways	24
The Process of Internalization	41
Kabbalah, a Judaism of Myth and Symbol	55
From Kabbalah to Hasidism	69
The Divergence of East and West and the Zionism of Each	86
1967, Victory and Defeat	101
2025: Where We Stand Today	114
Response	120
Acknowledgments	140

A Note About the Transliteration

I have adopted the following system of transliteration that allows me to distinguish between the following consonants in rendering Hebrew or Aramaic phrases:

’ = א   ‘ = ע   ḥ = ח   kh = כ

Prologue

I

There used to be a well-known joke among American Jews that went like this:

A young rabbi was invited as a candidate for a position in a new congregation. When he got there, the chairman of the search committee asked him: "What are you going to speak about?" The rabbi said, "I thought I'd speak about Shabbos, the beauty and importance of observing the Sabbath." "No," the chairman said "That's too controversial. Nobody here keeps Shabbos." "Then maybe I'll speak about kashrus," said the rabbi, the meaning of keeping a kosher home. "No no, rabbi. That's even worse. Hardly anyone here has a kosher home." "What then should I speak about?" asked the rabbi. "Well, you know, speak about *Judaism*."

2025 Update:
"I thought I'd speak about "Thou shalt not commit murder." Or maybe "Thou shalt not steal."
"No, no, rabbi, that's too controversial…Speak about *Judaism*. Maybe about the Sabbath."

II

Judges 16:27-31

Samson, our first Jewish Superhero, blinded, is taken by the Philistines to their capital, Gaza. Standing at its Temple, the House of their god Dagon, he flexes his muscles against its two central pillars and brings it crashing down, killing everyone inside, including himself. His family have to dig his body out of the rubble to bury him.

2025 Update:

Our current Superhero, the Israeli army, blinded by its civilian leaders, has once again flexed its muscles and brought down the House in Gaza—*nearly every house*. The question is whether *our* whole House—everything the Jewish people has stood for and created over the course of three thousand years—will also be buried under Gaza's rubble.

Preface

This has not been an easy book to write. Jews are used to being under threat from the outside. We have lived with all kinds of enemies for a couple of thousand years. A great scholar a while ago referred to us "The Ever Dying People," meaning that each generation of Jews thought it might be the last. We're a tough bunch when it comes to survival.

But here I'm speaking of a very different threat. My question is **Can Judaism be saved *from itself*?** Or from the worst and most dangerous currents within itself, carried forth from all those many generations of oppression and having echoed so loudly again in the Holocaust. Those worst elements within our collective memory have come to the surface, especially in Israel, since the 1967 conquest of Jerusalem and the West Bank. They have come to ring a hundred times more loudly since the terrible event of October 7, 2023. As of this writing, they are taking a dominant role in the shaping of Israeli government policy, accompanied by a loud demand that world Jewry sign on, supporting the Jewish state, whatever it does. This book is the cry of a Jew and a rabbi who refuses to sign.

This is a hard book to write for another reason as well. I am about to "wash a lot of dirty linen" in public here.

I worry that in doing so I might be seen as giving ammunition to the antisemites, the last thing we Jews need to do right now. I fear that some may type me as a *moser*, a traitor or informant against the Jews. I do not take this possible accusation lightly. But, having thought about it long and hard, I think it important in our day that certain elements within our tradition be faced and confronted directly, rather than being left hidden. I fear that today they no longer just fester, but are out there doing real harm, possibly even threatening our very existence as a moral force in the world. To confront them, we need to acknowledge their presence.

This book was written during the terrible summer of 2025. As it goes to press, we are celebrating the release of the hostages; a great moment indeed. Hopefully it will be followed by disarmament of Hamas and first steps in the rebuilding of Gaza. But the essential question raised by this book, the relationship between Jewish/Israeli nationalism and exclusivist elements within the Jewish tradition, remains the same.

One more note: When I use the "We" form in this book, it refers to us Jews, all of us. I believe strongly in the rabbinic dictum that "All Israel are responsible for one another." "Israel" in that ancient sentence meant Jews, not Israelis. But now it has come to mean that all of us, like it or not, bear some responsibility for Israel, the state, as well.

Introduction

It was 1961. I was all of 20 years old, a college senior and president of student Hillel at Brandeis University. I was thrilled to be engaged in deep conversation with Rabbi Zalman Schachter, whom I had invited to spend a weekend on our campus. He was just on his way out of being a traditional Chabad Hasid, on his way to becoming the key figure of a Neo-Hasidic revival within Judaism. I had just gotten over a period of rather self-punishing Orthodoxy in my adolescent years, followed by a sharp rebellion against it. I was well on my way toward my lifelong journey as a Jewish seeker. I had met Reb Zalman earlier and I knew that he could be an important guide in finding my path. Amid many other things he said, long forgotten, he spoke one sentence that has remained with me over these more than 60 years. It was in Yiddish, a language we both understood and valued, even though most of our conversation took place in English. *"Yiddishkeyt iz a derekh in avoyde,"* he said. Judaism is a way of service, of serving God.

That is how I have understood Judaism over the course of all these decades. It is a path, a way of approaching a life of service to the divine, to that which is holy, to the mysterious One. Reb Zalman did not use a term for God in that sentence; it was understood. He and I would both have preferred the unpronounceable Hebrew Y-H-W-H to the English G-O-D, but we understood what we meant. Devotion, inwardness, a desire to serve, open-heartedness, and "cultivation of the inner life" were all terms that characterized the spiritual path of which we were speaking, in a conversation that continued over many years. *Yiddishkeyt* or "Judaism" is a language in which to express that path. It is not the only such language or even necessarily the world's best. But it is *ours*; it is the language our heart speaks, the spiritual legacy of our ancestors implanted within us. That is what remained—and still remains, sixty years later—important to me.

Use of the term *Yiddishkeyt* in this context was entirely natural for Reb Zalman, as one who had spent his formative years within a Hasidic community. But in a broader context, its use becomes more complicated. Is it to be translated "Judaism" or "Jewishness?" There once was a whole world of people out there who rejected quite thoroughly any sort of religious faith, that which they would have called "Judaism," but affirmed precisely *Yiddishkeyt* as an alternative to it. The term vaguely described a set of values, including a special concern for fellow Jews and their fate as well as a certain affection for the traditional old-world Jewish way of life, without actually practicing any of its specific dictates. *Yiddishkeyt* was understood in those circles as something different from "Judaism."

When I was growing up there were lots of such people. Some of them were even members of my own extended family. Today, they have retreated to a small sect of ideologically driven Yiddishists. The great majority of those who might once have belonged to that camp now just call themselves Jewish non-believers. When asked the "religion" question on a Pew survey form they check off "none." But they still have a sense of Jewish identity, strong or weak. The vacuum created by the absence of religious faith was largely taken up by Zionism, which they see as a commitment to the Jews as a people, expressed mainly by love and support for the State of Israel.

It did not have to have happened that way. Jews have always had a strong sense of commitment to their fellow Jews, borne along and regularly reinforced by our long history of suffering. Such a sense of Jewish ethnicity or peoplehood might have sufficed to replace traditional religion for generations of nonbelievers. The problem for survival of Jewry here was that ethnicities not reflected in the color of one's skin do not do very well in the United States. On US government census forms, which ask if you are Black, Latino, or Pacific Islander, there is no place to write "Jewish" except under "religion." Nor is there a place to write "Italian-American" or "Polish-American." Those forms of identity are just not considered important. We all speak English at home and root for the same sports teams. For many, regional identity within the United States becomes more important than identification with the country or countries from which one or more of one's great-grandparents emigrated.

But for Jews, this decline in ethnic distinctiveness in America came at the worst possible time. The children and grandchildren of Jewish immigrants from Eastern Europe stood by and watched in horror as two thirds of the Jews remaining in Europe, one third of the entire Jewish people, were brutally and indiscriminately slaughtered. Although they mostly chose not to talk about it, every Jewish immigrant, including my own grandparents, remembered people who had been left behind and died in the pits or the gas chambers, whether they were siblings, cousins, childhood friends, or onetime neighbors. For the survivors themselves, of course, that was all much more vivid and debilitating. The plague of unspoken trauma and survivor guilt, passed from one generation to the next, did (and does) not allow most American Jews to feel comfortable with just forgetting the past and trying to fit into the New World we have been privileged to inherit.

Zionism stepped into that breach and became a surrogate religion. For a great many American Jews, support of Israel offered a link to one's Jewish identity that could be expressed by underwriting an active Jewish life for other people, living in a land far away. One could be supportive of Jewishness for someone else, for those who chose to live in Israel. Weren't they doing such a great job of building a new and free society, welcoming victims of anti-Jewish persecution from around the world? We should be supporting that! In this way, an American Zionist could express a loyalty to the Jewish people that did not impinge on their own full assimilation to the American Way of Life, including worship at the idolatrous Temple of "Success," the god of the American Dream.

Of course, the lines between these forms of religious and secular self-definition are never absolute. Jews who see themselves as secular may still attend a Passover Seder and light Hanukkah candles. The message in these events, however, is often secularized. The American secular seder, if it has any meaning beyond a great family gathering and dinner, is often similar to the seder of many Israelis. It is more a celebration of the liberation from Auschwitz and the establishing of the Jewish state than it is a memory of our bondage in ancient Egypt and redemption by divine hand. If slavery is mentioned, it immediately calls for the singing of "Go Down, Moses," better known to the participants than the traditional Hebrew songs for the occasion. Hanukkah makes it in America as a celebration of the very American value of religious liberty, even for those who reject religion. It is also, of course, a celebration of the victory of Jews over their more numerous and better armed foes, a story that immediately evokes 1948.

That replacement of Judaism, defined as a religion or a path of devotion, with Zionism, a proud feeling that Israel, especially a strong Israel, was "good for the Jews," became the "civil religion" of the organized Jewish community. Defending Israel, no matter what it did, became the first commandment of that religion. Synagogues and rabbis, too, were expected to participate enthusiastically in this task, in addition to—and sometimes even in defiance of—whatever other religious values they might hold.

This civil religion seemed to work well for many, until 2023.

Due to actions, statements, and intentions of the Israeli government, it is now in steep and rapid decline, especially for the younger generations. For them, 1945, 1948, and 1967 are nothing more than dates in history. Many within those generations, including some with strong Jewish education and commitment, have been deeply shocked and wounded, horrified by the behavior of the Israeli political leadership over the past several years. Outrage over the unfair and unequal treatment of Palestinians, which in fact has been going on for decades, was followed by a government-sponsored attempt to thwart democratic values and guarantees of an independent judiciary. It all felt too familiar to Jews living in the era of Donald Trump.

The Israeli reaction to the truly horrific massacre of October 7, 2023, made things much worse. The widespread impression, conveyed rather clearly by the Western news media, and confirmed by the vigorous Israeli protest movement, was that neither the government nor the army leadership (I do not speak here of individual soldiers, draftees who represent the full spectrum of views) care very much about the lives of Palestinians. This has been witnessed both by the massive bombing and destruction in Gaza and the cynical use and withholding of humanitarian aid as a weapon of war. Most recently, it is evidenced in the pathetic and ridiculous-sounding denial, by various Israeli spokesmen, that there is any hunger in Gaza. It's all a "blood libel," stemming from the world's bitter antisemitic bias. Esau hates Jacob.

All of this needs to be said with more than a nod to the complexity of the situation. Hamas is the first villain here, not only for October 7, but for its indifference to the lives of the Gazan people ever since it came to power. It took countless millions of dollars meant to feed and clothe the needy, or to build industry, and used it for underground tunnels from which it hoped to launch a messianic war against Israel. With regard to aid, it is true that the UNWRA system of distribution relied on Hamas, helping to keep it in power over a desperate and hungry population. But none of these real facts should be used to allow Israel to escape or deny its own degree of responsibility.

Bezalel Smotrich's policy goal, with Netanyahu's full assent, now seems fairly obvious.[1] It is a tactic I recall from studying *halakhah* called "You force him until he says, 'I want to!'"[2] The plan is to make the lives of the Palestinians so utterly miserable that they will eventually be desperate enough to leave the country "voluntarily," even going to the most awful of places. You can debate forever whether this is to be called "genocide," but it can surely be called *rish'ut*, wickedness, or evil. And it is being done in our name, that of the Jewish People. (My worst fear is that Trump, Kushner, and Huckabee are silently in on this idea.)

It is hard not to consider these acts by Israel, the excessive bombing and the delay of humanitarian aid, including food for the desperately hungry, to be war crimes. Quite a few young Israelis of conscience struggle with the question of whether to refuse to serve in the armed forces (very few do, in the end). Older reservists, who have suffered terrible amounts of burden and loss in this seemingly endless war, are refusing in larger numbers. Young diaspora Jews who have been raised in a surrogate religion of loyalty to Israel find themselves in a state of shock, questioning the belief in Israel's righteousness that was taken for granted in their parents' generation. At the age of 84, I find myself to be one of those "young people."

I have been a Zionist since I was about 10 years old (1951!), watching Abba Eban speak before the UN. I am old enough to remember Jews in the DP camps after the war looking for a place to go. I have a still earlier memory of my mother and

---

[1] As of this writing in September 2025. Nothing would make me happier than being proven wrong.
[2] Baba Batra 47b-48a; RaSHI to Lev. 1:3.

grandmother going through lists of Holocaust survivors in the Yiddish and English newspapers, looking in vain for relatives. I thus cannot join the chorus of the new diasporists, ready to put Zionism aside and, presumably, leave Israel to its fate. I remain committed to the idea of a Jewish state. Antisemitism, including the persecution of Jews for the crime of being Jews, is still a real enough possibility in our world to require a Jewish homeland, a refuge for those who need it. (This is quite different from the current Law of Return, which I oppose, encouraging all Jews to "ascend" or "redeem themselves" by moving to Israel.)

I wrote to a friend in Tel Aviv recently: "I still believe in a Jewish state, both in its legitimacy and the need for one. If you see a Jewish state anywhere, please let me know. I haven't seen one lately." It is hard for me to say that Israel is acting in any way I can recognize as the behavior of a Jewish state. Not in Gaza; not in Sdeh Teman, the notorious prison for Gazan terrorists; not across the West Bank.

For good reason, Zionism as the key expression of *Yiddishkeyt* for Jews who see themselves as non-religious is suddenly being called into question. Does being a Zionist these days involve some complicity with what Israel is doing? If so, can we really continue to be "believers?" For many Jews who attend synagogue as well, the strong Zionist component in their faith has been deeply shaken. Wasn't Judaism supposed to teach that every human being is the image of God and is to be treated that way? If that's what we believe, how can the government of a Jewish State be starving children? How can ministers of a Jewish State be championing ethnic cleansing? Do the Ten Commandments mean nothing to those violent settlers on the West Bank, who seem to regularly violate the prohibitions against both theft and murder? How can there be Jews, usually seen wearing *kippot* and *tsitsit*, attacking, even burning, Arab villages, or stealing sheep from their flocks?

Or do their actions in fact stem from a very different reading of the Jewish tradition itself, one of which we were barely aware? In this Judaism, God's election of Israel is not a call to service but a declaration of superiority. Either God chose us because we are somehow "better," more fully human, than others, or God's choosing us made us that way. In either case, we are the ones who are destined to rule, especially in the Land of Israel. Are there Jews who think of our shared legacy as one that calls us to a life of mastery (*ribbonut* in Hebrew, a word never found in classical Jewish sources) and conquest, rather than devotion and generosity? Apparently so, and quite a few of them. Could it be their understanding of Judaism itself that is leading at least to indifference to the subjugation and dehumanization of "lesser" human beings? We were never told about such Jews, but suddenly they seem to have come out of the woodwork, as it were, and have become the dominant force in Israeli leadership. The self-proclaimed leadership of "organized Jewry" in the United States has done very little to stand up to them. The ethic of supporting Israel, right or wrong, still seems to dominate, even as the news grows worse and worse.

American and other diaspora rabbis and educators are perhaps the most caught on the horns of this dilemma. They are people who take the moral teachings of Judaism seriously and try to get people to live by them. At the same time, they are seen as leaders of the Jewish people and are expected to show loyalty to Israel, the great collective project of the Jewish people over the past eighty years. Many of them are agonizing in their hearts, sympathizing with the deep questioning of Israel's actions expressed by younger Jews, but not daring to speak out about it because leaders within their congregations are also active in AIPAC or Jewish Federations, which still expect unquestioning loyalty to Israel, whatever it does.

Where do we go from here? That is the central question of the book before you. In order to examine it, we will need to travel through the course of Jewish spiritual and intellectual history, paying special attention to the interweaving of these two forms of *Yiddishkeyt*, the devotional and the ethno-national. Can they be separated from one another in anything that will still be recognizable as Judaism? Should they be? Where did this "shadow side" of Judaism come from? Have the national elements within our tradition been so corrupted by Israel's governmental policies and by the "Settler Judaism" it supports as to make them intolerable for people committed to what we see as the highest values of the Jewish tradition itself? Can we wash off the moral stain that Israel's behavior and our complicit silence have inflicted upon us, or will it stick forever? Can Judaism cleanse itself of the racism and condescension toward others that characterize the way it is so often invoked and sullied by the elected leaders of what still dares to call itself a "Jewish State," even as it wanders so far from behavior or values that we think of as "Jewish"?

To ask it differently, and perhaps even more controversially, have we "bet the whole dime," meaning the entire existence of Judaism as a moral and religious force in the world, on the Jewish State? Now that leadership of that state has fallen into the hands of politicians who represent the worst, rather than the best, of "Jewish values," we are forced to consider that once unaskable question. Xenophobia and exclusivism seem to have overridden love of humanity and an attempt to make the world a better place. We had thought Judaism was about service, to God and all of God's creation. That meant both celebrating all of life and working to eliminate human suffering.

Over against these, there has emerged a Judaism—or a "Jewishness"[3] that is about preserving the self-interest and privilege of Jews, especially in the Holy Land. Acts of violence and land-grabbing are daily occurrences, cloaked under the mantle of "defense."

---

[3] I will not call it *yiddishkeyt*; here Yiddish remains *loshn koidesh*.

The Israeli army, supposedly committed to *tohar ha-neshek*, "purity of arms," has repeatedly been shown to be at least indifferent to these crimes, and sometimes directly involved in them. Arrest and punishment of those who commit acts of anti-Palestinian violence is rare.

Many who serve within the Israeli army are aware of this. Some have even dared to speak of it publicly. The poor Israeli conscripts and reservists, exhausted by terribly extended military service, many traumatized by the awful things they've seen and done, are also victims of this conflict. They too deserve our sympathy, alongside the much worse suffering Palestinian victims.

You might say, of course, that all this was dictated by the Holocaust. We became so frightened, understandably, that all we wanted to do was to survive. Self-protection, surely understandably, became our goal. A strong Israel, featuring a powerful military, was the vehicle for that survival. The IDF as our Superhero. Nothing else mattered. Any threat to that quite literally drove us crazy. Our Arab enemies played right into that by threatening to utterly destroy us. On October 7, 2023, they acted on that threat.

But now we are being forced to reflect. What have we done to others—and to ourselves—in the name of that survival? I hear our ancient sage Hillel shouting in my ear: *"Do not do to another what you would hate having done to you. That is the whole Torah; the rest is commentary."*[4] I hear that, I look at Gaza, and I shudder. If that is what Judaism has become, are we not giving to Hitler the ultimate posthumous victory? Into what have we transformed ourselves?

Yes, I am quite aware what *they* would have done to *us* had the situation been reversed. Indeed, they showed us precisely that on October 7. But that is not the point of Hillel's teaching and it should not be used as an excuse to undercut it.

---

[4] Shabbat 31a.

The author of these words is not interested in being remembered as a lone and lonely moral voice, even one praised for its courage, as such voices often are. This book is a call for nothing less than a *crusade*, a word that we Jews do not use lightly. I am calling upon those who think as I do to put on our intellectual and spiritual armor and *fight*, using all our intellectual and spiritual tools, to preserve what we know is the best of our tradition. To do this, we will need to set our lesser differences aside (including that oh-so-precious line between Orthodoxy and heterodoxy), in order to rescue the Torah, our maiden in deep distress, from the clutches of the "Other Side."

To do that, we need to understand something of our history, focused on the ways that history has shaped our present conflict. I ask you to accompany me on a brief (and therefore necessarily simplified) journey through Jewish history, with an emphasis on certain key ideas. We will pay special attention to the tension between the twin themes of a Judaism that celebrates God as Author of Creation, worshipped by all, and the special role we claim as God's partners in a unique covenant. Both of these religious themes have existed against the all-too-real background of the Jewish people's struggle for survival in an often hostile world and the ways, not always so beautiful, in which that struggle has shaped us.

Our Biblical Legacy

Ancient Israel was composed of a group of tribes that in the course of what we call the biblical period came to define themselves as a single people. The narratives around the patriarchs, culminating in the story of Jacob and his sons, describe that sense of a retrojected common ancestry, alongside reasons for hostility toward those outside the emerging confederation. It is only after their descent into Egypt and in the course of their enslavement, in the first chapter of the Book of Exodus, where the word "people" is first used in describing the Israelites. It was their memory of shared oppression that forged them into a nation.

Whether that memory is historical or not is much debated by biblical era historians. No archaeological or documentary evidence (outside of the Bible itself) has been produced attesting to the enslavement of Israel in Egypt or to the Exodus. But whatever the historicity, the collective memory of those events was highly formative to the identity of the nation that emerged from them. Israelites saw themselves as descendants of liberated slaves. The great revelation at Sinai opens with the sentence "I am Y-H-W-H your God who brought you forth from the land of Egypt, from the house of bondage." The Torah frequently and famously calls upon the Israelites to treat strangers and aliens in their midst with kindness "because you were strangers in the land of Egypt." That is a memory never to be forgotten.

The greatest and most lasting ritual innovation of biblical religion is the institution of the weekly Sabbath, on which all Israelites, and also their servants, were allowed the privilege of rest. This was a tremendous innovation, one that marked and defined the Israelite and then the Jewish people throughout history. In the religions of the ancient near east, rest belonged to the gods. Humans were created in order to serve them, so that they would not need to hunt for their food, but would be able to rest in godly pleasure. Kings, as sons of the gods, were also sometimes allowed to rest. They too had slaves to wait on their needs. But the idea that the entire people would be treated this way was an innovation of Israelite religion. Who would think of such a thing, if not the descendants of slaves, precisely those people who have never been given, but longed for, the privilege to rest?

The Sabbath is first mentioned at the beginning of the second chapter of Genesis, immediately following the six-day creation of the world. The crown of creation, in that narrative, is the human being, created, according to Genesis 1:28, "in the image and likeness of God." That, too, is a great innovation of Israel's religious genius. Again, a description of privilege that once belonged to kings is now given to all humanity. We are *all* God's children, carrying forward the image and likeness of our Father/Creator. When Genesis 2:7 offers the account of God's blowing the breath of life into Adam's nostrils, the famous medieval commentator Nahmanides adds, "Whoever blows breath into another's nostrils, it is his own breath that he blows." Every human being, the descendent of Adam/Eve, bears the Divine breath within their soul.

The placing of these two events, the creation of humans and the first Sabbath, next to each other is hardly coincidental. Even though the Sabbath of Genesis is about God's resting, rather than that of humans, the point is clear. There cannot be a living creature bearing the image of God who is not allowed to rest. It is the right to rest, to get off the treadmill of earning a livelihood on a weekly basis, that gives us the ability to reflect upon and develop the Divine image within us. To say it in the traditional language of Judaism, *menuḥah* precedes *kedushah*; rest and the reflection it permits allow us to seek out holiness, the goal of religious living.

What we see emerging in ancient Israel is a universalist faith engendered by a particular tribe or nation. The narrative of Genesis clearly implies that the Divine image, the breath of God, and the legacy of the Sabbath belong to all humanity. But the bearers of this truth are the Israelites, a nation struggling to discover and assert its own identity while surrounded by hostile forces, other peoples and tribes competing for the same piece of land and its scant resources.

This dual legacy will follow Israel, later defined as the Jewish people, throughout its history. It is still that which torments us today. What are we Jews? A religious community with a universal message or a people coming in the name of *our* God to stake our own claim among the nations? Is it even remotely possible to be both of these at the same time? How could that possibly work?

The covenant and revelation at Sinai are taken within Judaism to be the very basis of our collective religious existence. As we stood, all of us, men, women, and children, before the mountain, we were declared by God to be "a kingdom of priests and a holy nation." This is the famous Election of Israel. Although the term *baḥar*, "choosing," is not used here, this becomes the basis for the nation of Israel as God's "Chosen People." What is often ignored when this passage is quoted is the centrality of **priesthood** in what I take to be ancient Israel's clearest statement of self-definition. The priest exists to serve both God and community. Frequently he is the intermediary between the two, bringing the needs of the community before God and teaching that community to follow the divine will. If Israel declares itself to be taking on this unique function of an entire nation of priests, clearly the community it serves is that of the rest of humanity. *Israel's "chosenness" is a gift of service, not of privilege.*

This Sinai-based sense of religious mission to define the people of Israel stands alongside the ancient tribal legacy. God's promise to give to the descendants of Abraham, Isaac, and Jacob the land where they first settled is repeated frequently in the Torah text, especially in Deuteronomy. The word *nishbaʿ* is often used in this context; God "promised" or even "swore" to the ancestors that their offspring would have this land. Interestingly, however, the notion of chosenness (*beḥirah, segulah*) never is invoked in that context. The two legacies, that of ethnic descent and promise of the land, and that of priesthood and holiness, exist side by side, but are not to be confused or combined. Abraham has a covenant and a promise, but only at Sinai do we become a *goy kadosh*, a holy nation. And that goes right along with our priesthood.

The word *ʿeved* in ancient Hebrew is rendered in English as both "slave" and "servant;" the language knows no distinction between these two. *ʿAvodah* (yes, that was *avoyde* in the Yiddish transliteration) means "servitude" or "bondage." We are brought forth from Egypt, from bondage to other humans, in order to become servants of Y-H-W-H. But there is an important difference between our bondage to Pharaoh and our service of Y-H-W-H. Israel's relationship with God is covenantal, an agreement between two parties. In a stunningly powerful ceremony (apparently his own creation; he is nowhere commanded to do this) described in Exodus 24, Moses orders the slaughter of a dozen bullocks. He has the "youth of Israel" gather the blood of these animals in buckets. Moses then takes the buckets and pours half the blood over the altar, representing God, and splashes the other half out over the people. It is as though he is saying, *You, Y-H-W-H and Israel, are now blood brothers. Nothing can ever separate you.*

Israel are to see themselves, from that moment, as both servants and partners of God in the world. Their duties in that relationship are best summed up by the Deuteronomist, speaking in the voice of Moses' charge to Israel before his death:

> Now, Israel, what does Y-H-W-H your God ask of you, but that you fear Y-H-W-H your God, walk in all His ways, and love Him, serving Y-H-W-H your God with all your heart and soul. (Deut. 10:12)

Two notes on key words in this verse: *Yir'ah*, "fear," has a wide range of meanings. Later Jewish writings repeatedly make it clear that "standing in awe" is part of that range. Only for the child does it mean fear of punishment. In an adult religion, it ranges from fearing the loss of intimacy with Y-H-W-H to standing in awe at the magnificence of God's presence throughout Creation. "Walking" in God's ways gives us the term *halakhah*, often (unfortunately, I think) translated "Jewish law," but really meaning "walking the path."

The religion of ancient Israel was one lived fully within the confines of this world. Some have seen it as a reaction against the religious aura of ancient Egypt, where life in this world was entirely a period of preparation for true life in the world to come. There is almost nothing said of the afterlife in the entire Hebrew Bible, except for a few scattered references to a place called *She'ol*, the neutral and somewhat uninteresting place where souls apparently reside after death. There is no sense of reward or punishment in the afterlife. The nature of reward for living the good life is very clearly set out in Scripture, here quoted from the second paragraph included in the daily calling out of the *Shema'* ("Hear, O Israel!"):

> If you faithfully obey the commands I am giving you today—to love the Lord your God and to serve Him with all your heart and with all your

soul, I will send rain to your land in its season, both autumn and spring rains, so that you may gather in your grain, new wine and olive oil. I will provide grass in the fields for your cattle, and you will eat and be satisfied. (Deut. 11:13-15)

Such a religion works best, of course, when verified by prosperity. In times of suffering, including especially the droughts and famines that often ravished the ancient near east, it was significantly more problematic. Ultimately, the author of Job gave the lie to the Deuteronomic promise. Writing, perhaps, in a somewhat later and less fortunate era, as well as surely reflecting on his own experience of life in God's world, he made it clear that the righteous cannot count on reward and that there is no justice apparent in this life. Job's "friends" tried to console him and argue with him at the same time. Their message includes reference to the idea of reward in the afterlife, but Job dismisses this as an avoidance of the real issue of the human being's arbitrary fate. The creators of the biblical canon had the courage to include this rather heretical book, alongside Ecclesiastes, but the emerging religion of Second Temple Judaism and the proto-rabbinic tradition did not take their message fully to heart. Job is not an easy book to live with. Perhaps fortunately, the Hebrew text was so difficult that its message remained rather obscure.

The universalization of Israelite monotheism was a long and complicated process, by no means developing in a straight linear pattern. In one of the oldest biblical texts we have, Moses' Song at the Sea in Exodus 15, Y-H-W-H is clearly the "Man of war," leading His people in battle against their enemies, defeating even the mighty gods of Egypt. Other early texts see Him as giving this land to Israel as other gods have given territory to their own peoples (Judges 11:24). It was in the prophetic period, the 7th–5th centuries BCE, when a more universal notion of divinity emerged. Y-H-W-H was the Creator of the entire world and was therefore the God of all people, indeed the author of nature itself. This is probably the setting in which such great creation hymns as Psalms 104 and 148 were written. This was probably when an old tribal name for divinity was analogized to the verb *h-w-h*, "to be," meaning that Y-H-W-H included being in all its tenses, the God of past, present, and future. This gave us the famous play on the name (Exodus 3:14) in which Y-H-W-H refuses to define Himself, saying *Ehyeh asher Ehyeh*, "I am what I am" or "I shall be whatever I shall be."

Perhaps the finest and most outspoken definition of the universality of Israel's God was that spoken by the prophet Malachi (1:11), who lived at the beginning of the Second Temple period.

> From the place where the sun rises to where it sets, My name is great among the nations. In every place there are incense and sacrifice to My name. These are pure offerings, for My name is great among the nations.

A psalmist of the same era (113:3) wrote "From the place where the sun rises to where it sets, the name of Y-H-W-H is praised." These writers knew full well that the name Y-H-W-H was used only in Israel and was not known throughout the world. What they are saying is that all names of God are one. Whatever God is called, people everywhere are worshiping the same One whom we Israelites know as Y-H-W-H, the God of Israel.

That was indeed quite a radical innovation. In its ideal form, it should have meant that the entire zero sum game among religions makes no sense. Had it been allowed to stand alone, an awful lot of suffering in the course of Israel's future history and that of humanity in general could have been avoided. But, of course, that was not to be the case. Y-H-W-H as the old tribal God, the one who battles for His people against other gods and nations, the One who promised us the Land, did not vanish. "He" co-existed within the same divine Self as the universal deity, the one beyond all names and limits. Hence our problem.

The Torah text as we have received it is a weaving together of different voices, different witnesses to the history of ancient Israel and the ongoing development of its relationship both with Y-H-W-H and with the nations among whom it lived. So too the later canonization process of the TaNaKh, or Hebrew Bible. The genius of the canon is that it did not have to smooth out all the dissonance within it. The message of one verse, story, or even entire book of the Bible might well stand in contrast to that of another. The collective mind of the canonizers was broad enough to include them all.

As Second Temple Judaism developed, especially following the Hasmonean victory in the mid-second century BCE, quite a few non-Jews were attracted to the universalist teachings of Israel. Some of them visited the Temple in Jerusalem, which was known to have an outer courtyard designated for "those who fear the Lord," meaning non-Israelites who were nevertheless devotees. Some of these presumably became full converts to Judaism, as both the very notion of Judaism as a religion and the possibility of conversion to it began to emerge. Others undoubtedly remained close to the teachings but did not convert. Surely, some among them became the first gentile followers of Christianity as it began to emerge in the late first century of the common era.

The tension between the two types of Judaism I have been describing here may be seen in a comparative look at two well-known compositions in the Book of Psalms, Psalm 136 and Psalm 145. The former, known in Jewish liturgy as *hallel ha-gadol*, "the great praise," had the Temple congregation shouting out "His compassion endures forever!" as a refrain following each line, probably chanted by the Levites. Although opening in praise of Creation, it becomes a fully nationalist anthem, praising God for destroying our enemies and awarding us their lands:

> He struck down the firstborn of Egypt.
> His compassion endures forever.
>
> And brought Israel out from among them.
> His compassion endures forever.
>
> With a mighty hand and outstretched arm;
> His compassion endures forever.
>
> He split the Reed Sea asunder,
> His compassion endures forever.
>
> And brought Israel through its midst,
> His compassion endures forever.
>
> He swept Pharaoh and his army into the Reed Sea;
> His compassion endures forever.
>
> He led his people through the wilderness;
> His compassion endures forever.
>
> Striking down great kings,
> His compassion endures forever.
>
> And killing mighty kings—
> His compassion endures forever.
>
> Sihon king of the Amorites,
> His compassion endures forever.

> And Og king of Bashan—
> His compassion endures forever.
>
> Giving their land as an inheritance,
> His compassion endures forever.
>
> An inheritance to his servant Israel.
> His compassion endures forever...

If all these deeds are testaments to God's ḥesed, it of course means that such compassion is directed toward Israel alone.

Compare this fiercely nationalist song with another psalm, also famous in the context of Jewish liturgy. This is Psalm 145, known to Jews as *Ashrey*, due to the two verses later (in early rabbinic times) attached to its beginning. The psalm itself contains not a single reference to anything that might be called "Jewish" or "Israelite" in the specific sense—no mention of Jerusalem, Zion, the Temple, or the Israelite people. It is a universalist hymn of praise to God, written in beautiful late biblical Hebrew, following an alphabetical acrostic pattern. Notice in the passage quoted (verses 9-21) how many times the author uses the word "all," here highlighted:

> Y-H-W-H is good to *all*;
> He has compassion on *all* He has made.
>
> *All* your works praise you, O Y-H-W-H;
> Your devotees extol You.
>
> They tell of the glory of Your kingdom
> and speak of Your might,

so that the children of Adam may know of Your
    mighty acts
and the glorious splendor of Your kingdom.

Your kingdom is an everlasting kingdom,
and Your dominion endures through *all*
    generations.

Y-H-W-H upholds *all* who fall
and lifts up *all* who are bowed down.

The eyes of *all* look to You,
and You give them their food at the proper time.

You open Your hand
and satisfy the desires of ***all living things***.

Y-H-W-H is righteous in *all* His ways
and faithful in *all* He does.

Y-H-W-H is near to *all* who call on Him,
to *all* who call on Him in truth.

He fulfills the desires of those who fear Him;
He hears their cry and saves them.

Y-H-W-H watches over *all* who love him,
but *all* the wicked he will destroy.

My mouth will speak in praise of Y-H-W-H.
Let ***all flesh*** praise His holy name
for ever and ever.

This author is perhaps even more strikingly universal than his colleague quoted above is nationalistic. The constant repetition of the word "all" tells us again and again that he is *insisting* on this universalism. The references to "the children of Adam," "all living things," and "all flesh" make that completely clear. If you will forgive me a bit of fantasy, I picture these two psalmists sitting on opposite sides of a writing table in the scriptorium of the Second Temple. One is writing over and over again of the triumph of Israel's God over each enemy they have encountered along the road, justifying our claim to conquer and settle their lands. Divine "compassion" is all directed toward us, not toward our enemies. The author is the father of all those military chaplains through history who will assure the troops that "God is on our side!" The other hears him and wants to remind him just as frequently that Y-H-W-H is the God of *all, all, all*—not just Israel and its territorial aspirations.

Yes, I am saying that the conflict that is so tearing the Jewish people apart today has been with us for a very long time.

Judaism and Christianity: The Parting of the Ways

Rabbinic Judaism, the form of Jewish religion that has been practiced for the past two thousand years, began to emerge in the first century of the common era, both before and after the destruction of the Second Temple by the Roman armies in the year 70 CE. It stands in a complicated relationship with the religion of ancient Israel, of which it claims to be the faithful continuation. In fact, the rabbis used great boldness in replacing and reinterpreting biblical traditions, while at the same time representing themselves as its teachers and preservers.

Much of ancient Israelite history may be depicted through three types of leaders who characterized it. Priests, kings, and prophets lived side by side and in frequent tension with one another. Each had its own account of the early history of Israel and the message it bore for present and future generations. Their differing societal functions led them to represent different values within the constellation of the nation's life. These are interwoven within the biblical narrative. Kings stood for political stability and military prowess, victory over Israel's enemies, both then and now. Priests represented the Temple cult, called the 'avodah, and devotion to God through it. They also represented religious authority. The prophet represented an ongoing voice of God, making demands of moral living that often challenged and impinged on the domains of both other sorts of leaders. The prophets denounced the authority of both kings and priests, seeing both, indeed all forms of human power, as capable of corruption.

With the final Roman conquest and the destruction of the Second Temple, kingship and priesthood lost their value. Both the House of David and the Hasmonean royal family essentially disappeared from the scene. There would be no more kings in Israel until the advent of Messiah, off in the distant future. Israel, we may say (actually Judea), ceased to exist as a political entity. So too, the power of the priest, no longer able to serve in his primary functions around the Temple cult and its offerings on the altar, became vestigial. Descendants of Aaron are still honored by being called first to read from the Torah and to bless the community. But their standing is a shadow of its former self, as your friend Mr. Cohen will tell you.

The early rabbis also proclaimed that prophecy had come to an end. As the canon was defined in the second century CE, the prophets of the early Second Temple period, some 500 years earlier, were declared as the last to be considered authoritative. This did not mean that the phenomenon of prophesying had disappeared from Israel. The latter-day forms of prophecy had much to do with visions of the heavens and declarations about the end of time. The very contemporary moral focus of the earlier prophets was shifted to concerns for the apocalypse and journeys into the heavens. But these teachings and writings (except for the Book of Daniel) were not included in the canon.

Two reasons for this rejection will tell us much about the mindset of the early rabbis. One was a concern for long-term survival of the community in the face of destruction and an emerging sense of "exile," even for those still living in the Holy Land. This new Judaism (unlike the emerging Christian Church) did not see itself as living in immediate anticipation of messianic redemption or the transformation of reality. The rabbis recalled themselves as having stood against those messianist rebels who had brought about the destruction. "The wicked kingdom of Rome" was likely to exist for a long time and the question was how to survive while living in its shadow. The story of Rabbi Yohanan ben Zakkai saying to the Roman general who destroyed Jerusalem "Give me Yavneh and its sages" became paradigmatic. The task of Judaism was to survive and to keep the light of its teachings burning in the midst of a dark world. Apocalyptic fantasies were only a distraction from this task. Hence they were not to be taken seriously.

Secondly, an ongoing sense of prophetic revelation would have undercut the authority of the emerging new class of Jewish leadership, one that had not existed in biblical times. The communities of rabbis and their circles of disciples who were creating the forms of disciplined observance that they felt would preserve both Jewry and Judaism over the long haul were quite distinct from those Jews who wrote and followed the tales of journeys to heaven that were also widespread at the time. The emerging rabbis (descended from the Pharisees) claimed authority via their scholarly credentials. They were the ones who knew, studied, and taught the traditions of ancient Israel. If God is continuing to offer new revelations, the value of knowing the old ones diminishes in importance. But if the canon is closed and all we have are the ancient words of God, nothing is more important than *knowledge*, which bestows the power and authority to interpret them. This belongs to ḤaZaL, our wise teachers, of blessed memory, the sages and their disciples in every generation.

The rabbinic claim to be the authentic continuation of biblical tradition stood in contrast to a new counterclaim that also emerged in the century following the Temple's destruction. At first, the followers of the would-be prophet from Nazareth were a small group, one among many sects that existed in the margins of the broader and ill-defined Jewish community. But after their refashioning by a religious genius called Paul, whose original name was Saul of Tarsus, Christianity became a very significant challenge indeed. Beginning in the later second century, much of what became rabbinic Judaism was defined in contrast to its increasingly serious rival claimant in interpreting what that group would come to see as the "Old Testament."

Paul, spiritual convert and successor to the emerging Gospel traditions, was a powerhouse of a theologian. He challenged the just now emerging rabbinic version of Judaism in two essential ways. First was the utter privatization of spirituality. In this new faith, you come before God, or "come to Christ," purely as an individual. You stand before God shorn of ancestry, economic status, ethnic or gender identity, family, and social context. "There is neither Jew nor Greek, there is neither slave nor free, no male or female, for you are all one in Christ Jesus (Galatians 3:28)." You come before God alone and naked to the core. You are no more or less than a single human being, standing alone. A "poor sinner" in the language of later Christianity. You then become part of an emerging new "one," the newborn Church, community of the faithful.

This stood in strong contrast to the then current Jewish (and emerging rabbinic) view that a Jew comes to stand before God in both vertical and horizontal contexts. You are a descendent of the patriarchs, whose merit protects you, and ancestor of many generations to come, Jews who will study Torah, keep the commandments, and await the final redemption. Your soul was present at Sinai, along with those of all future generations, and you affirmed the covenant. Your being a link in that chain is essential to your identity. You are also part of the holy people now scattered and wounded in exile, toward whom Y-H-W-H has declared His eternal and covenantal love.

Secondly, Paul viewed the entire biblical tradition in highly spiritualized terms. The Jews continued to follow the law of Moses, concerned about the details of proper observance as they were being defined in the first decades of the rabbinic period, following the great destruction. The emerging Christian community saw itself as able to follow the word of God, said Paul, through the faith of Abraham, which had preceded the commandments, and thus to do without all the outer forms of Jewish ritual life. Paul and other New Testament authors poked fun at the seeming pettiness of the rabbis' halakhic concerns. To follow God was to live in the spirit, not to observe the commandments. When the talmudic rabbis of the third or fourth century claimed that Abraham had observed all the commandments,[5] including prohibitions that the rabbis themselves had initiated, they meant to say that they recognized no such thing as faith without observance. Faith in God is vindicated by the following of God's teachings, and these include the practices that came to define Judaism. Proclamations of "faith" without praxis are vague and untethered. But Paul quoted Genesis 15:6: "Abraham had faith in Y-H-W-H and God considered that [sufficient] justification for him." "Justification through faith," the great slogan of the Protestant Reformation, begins in Paul's debate with the rabbis over that verse in the Torah.

The two faiths might be contrasted by just looking at their differing views of Abraham, patriarch for both. For the Christian, Abraham is the man of faith. This is seen both in the verse just quoted and in Genesis 22, the story of the binding of Isaac that Soren Kierkegaard, among the greatest of Christian theologians, read so seriously.[6] For the Jew, Abraham is father of the nation and the one to whom God said: "to your seed have I given this land" (Gen. 15:18). The binding of Isaac on the altar is central to the Jewish tradition as well, but there it is about the merits of our ancestors. It is also reminiscent of our long history of suffering and self-sacrifice. Its echoes continue to reverberate very loudly for Israeli parents in our time, both those who are sending their children off to war and those who have lost them in it. That is very different than Abraham as the Christian "knight of faith."

---

[5] Yoma 28b.
[6] In his *Fear and Trembling*.

This distinction between the two rival claimants' paths of carrying forth the Hebrew Bible's legacy led directly to the Christian stereotyping of Judaism as "the religion of the letter" of the law and Christianity as that of the spirit. This was to become an essential trope of the growing antisemitism or "anti-Judaism," that was inevitably created by classical Christian theology. But the rabbis very clearly declared "The Compassionate One seeks the heart"[7] and many other formulations parallel to it. A true follower of rabbinic tradition is to serve God "not in order to receive a reward,"[8] because the joy of fulfilling a mitzvah was itself all the reward one needed. *Ahavat Torah*, the love of learning, and *simḥah shel mitzvah*, the joy of fulfilling a commandment, lay at the heart of "spirituality" within the rabbinic tradition. This was a form of spirituality totally linked to the discipline of praxis, sometimes making it difficult for outsiders to perceive.

It is fair to say that both of these claimants were being honest and partially accurate in asserting to represent the fulfillment of Scriptural vision in their own day. But they weighted the various elements within the Hebrew Bible somewhat differently. One might say that the favorite Hebrew Bible books of early Christianity were Leviticus (with sacrifice—about to be transformed, but to remain crucial—and religious morality standing at its center) and Psalms, where the inner life of the individual found its best expression. For the rabbis, the favorite Scriptures were Exodus, the national narrative of the Jews, including both liberation and revelation, and Deuteronomy, combining fealty to praxis with a new vocabulary of religious emotion (*ahavah, yir'ah, devequt, ḥesheq*, etc.). It was these that had made the deepest impression.

The point is that every use of the past is a choice. This is true, as

---

[7] Sanhedrin 106b and RaSHI ad loc.
[8] M. Avot 1:3.

we have seen, within the biblical canon itself. But it is also true in the divergence between Christianity and Judaism, and then within the emerging complex faces of each of these traditions. Each developed out of an ongoing process of selection and reinterpretation of the texts and beliefs inherited from prior generations.

From its outset, Christianity was a religion concerned first and foremost with the question of salvation, meaning the redemption of lost souls, those of sinners. We were all sinners, beginning with Adam and Eve. The question "Are you saved?" became central to the emerging Christian consciousness, having everything to do with your future in the afterlife. Jews would never quite understand that question. Our question was rather "Are you living the good life?" meaning that of following the commandments and serving Y-H-W-H. If the answer was "Yes," reward might follow. But you were not supposed to be thinking about it.

The tension between national and religious elements within the tradition which I pointed out above by examining two psalms continued to find its articulation within the great rabbinic creation of *midrash* and *aggadah*, creative hermeneutics and narrative theology. The rabbis certainly affirmed Genesis 1:28, the creation of all humans in God's image, and made a point of emphasizing both the shared brotherhood of all people and the precious uniqueness of each individual. The second-century Mishnah, the first codification of Jewish practice, rarely makes theological assertions in a direct way. But it sets aside that hesitancy to declare:

> Why were humans created singly [i.e., all descended from a single couple]? To teach you that anyone who destroys one soul, Scripture ascribes him blame as if he destroyed an entire world. And anyone who sustains one soul, Scripture credits him as if he sustained an entire world.[9]

---

[9] Later manuscripts, including those from which early printed versions were

Another reason: This was in order to [bring about] peace among people, *so that no one could say to another: "My father is greater than your father."* And it was also so that the heretics [who believe in multiple gods] might not say: There are many authorities in Heaven, [and each created a different group of humans].

This also serves to tell of the greatness of the blessed Holy One. When a person stamps out multiple coins with one seal, they are all alike. But the supreme King of kings, the blessed Holy One, stamped all people with the seal of Adam, and not one of them is similar to another. Therefore, each and every person is obligated to say: "The world was created for me."[10]

This statement could well be taken as the credo of a universalist religious humanism. But the same tradition, in the same era, declares clearly that *"The world was created for the sake of Israel* [i.e., the Jewish people]."[11] It is by their merit that the world exists. "God set a condition upon creation. If Israel accept my Torah, all will be well. But if not, I will thereby return you all to primordial chaos."[12]

How do these two very divergent worldviews manage to coexist within the same tradition? We are not speaking only of universalist and particularist elements, which one might imagine as able to live side by side. But in these statements the universal

---

made, read "One soul of Israel" here and below. But scholarly research has shown that to have been an emendation. This original and more universalistic version is quoted also in the Qur'an.
[10] Mishnah Sanhedrin 4:5.
[11] Tanhuma Buber 3:67.
[12] Shabbat 88b.

itself is said to depend upon the particular! God not only has a special bond with Israel, the people who accepted His Torah. The entire world was created for their sake! If that is the case, all other peoples would seem, by definition, to have a secondary status in the eyes of their Creator. But how can that be if God created Adam singly "so that no one could say 'My father is greater than you father'"? We seem to have no choice but to say that there were divergent views within the circles of early rabbis, just as there were among Second Temple psalmists. The presence of divergent views, without the need to fully resolve them, we should recall, characterizes Judaism throughout the ages. ("Wherever you find two Jews, you find at least three opinions," as the saying goes.) The rabbis liked to say, regarding differing and conflicting opinions within the emerging *halakhah*: "Both these and those are the words of the living God."[13]

The notion that love and brotherhood form the very basis of what it means to be a religious person seems to have been a growing ideal in first-century Jewish circles. When Hillel, living in the last century before the common era, was approached by a would-be proselyte who asked him to "Teach me the entire Torah while I stand on one foot" he responded, "Do not do to another what you would hate having done to yourself. The rest is commentary. Go and learn!"[14] Jesus is quoted in the gospels as saying that the essence of Torah, "the old law," lies in the commandments to love God and love your neighbor.[15] Rabbi Akiva, in the early second century, is supposed to have said "'Love your neighbor as yourself' (Lev. 19:18) is the most basic rule of Torah." His friend Ben Azzai disputed that claim and said "I know a more basic rule than that. 'On the day that God created humans, He made them in

---

[13] 'Eruvun 13b, and frequently.
[14] Shabbat 31a.
[15] Matthew 22:37.

the divine image; male and female He created them.' (Gen. 5:1)."[16] We are not certain what Ben Azzai's argument with Akiva was about. But it may well be that he feared that "neighbor" could be limited to Jews alone. By placing the emphasis on the original creation of humans, he was insisting that it must apply universally.

The verse in the second chapter of Genesis that has God blowing His breath into Adam's nostrils opens with the word *va-yiytser*, "He created." The word is written in the Torah with a double *yod*, allowing the midrash to understand it to imply a double meaning. God created humans with a double *yetser*, or inclination of the heart.[17] From the moment of our creation, all of us humans have both good and evil urges within us. To be in God's image seems to imply freedom of moral choice. We have the power to be like God, who said the word "Good!" over each day's work in Creation. But we also have the freedom to transgress, to turn away from our Creator and His path of goodness. We are not condemned to be sinners in need of salvation, as the Church came to teach, but we have an even shot at making the right decisions, those that will keep us on the path of Torah. The "inner life" as described by the early rabbis is very much about those choices, with Torah and emerging *halakhah* to serve as guides toward the proper path. Religious life was more about behavior and learning than it was about faith.

Halakhah itself emerged in the form of an ongoing dialectic between diverse views and local traditions. We often see the rabbis accepting a current practice and then seeking to tie it to one biblical source or another. In early times, they did so with great bravado, seeking to make Scripture conform to their own views. As time went on, the tradition became more conservative and protective of that which had already been said. It is also clear that Jews in varying localities practiced their religion in a variety

---

[16] Yerushalmi Nedarim 9:6.
[17] Bereshit Rabbah 14:4.

of ways, seeing them as handed down from their ancestors. Only as the Diaspora widened and inter-communal communication improved were attempts made to unify and codify the system.

Over the century following the destruction of the Temple in the year 70 CE, the "Godfearers" who had visited its courtyards seem to have vanished. It is likely that many of them, alongside many Greek-speaking Jews in the western diaspora communities, joined the ranks of the first Christians. Once Paul made it clear that one did not have to be a Jew in order to enter the Church, which was in effect the Kingdom of Heaven, the community of the saved, Christianity became the more obvious choice. Part of the difference lay in the avoidance of the need to observe the practices of the Torah as they were being defined in the emerging rabbinic tradition. This was symbolized especially by the difficulty and embarrassment around circumcision. But it was also true that the Judeans were a defeated and disgraced people after the Roman armies had vanquished them. It was not easy to identify with such a people and to join its ranks. Christianity had no such requirement. "Neither Jew nor Greek" meant that you entered the church as an individual. You were not joining a tribe or a people, and your identity as a Roman or a Greek could in fact remain intact.

Christian privatization of individuals and their faith left "the old Israel" with its sense of peoplehood. Traditions, folkways, and memories of the people have enriched our lives and legacy beyond belief. But the dark side of our being a people is that all others were considered outsiders, less than welcome in our sacred places and moments except through the radical act of conversion, which came to mean joining the people and sharing in its fate as well as its faith.

For a further look at the ongoing tension between universalistic and national or exclusivist attitudes in rabbinic Judaism, we will again examine two selections of liturgy written in the rabbinic era. Remember that liturgical texts, by their very nature, were shared with the entire community of worshipers and were therefore in a position to be influential in both expressing and shaping religious attitudes in the community as a whole. These were sometimes more important, in that sense, than statements to be found in more obscure midrashic or talmudic bodies of writing.

Our first text is an early and anonymous *piyyut* or liturgical poem called *Ve-Ye'etayu* ("They Shall Come!"), still a highlight of the High Holy Day liturgy, usually sung with great gusto. It was most likely composed in the Land of Israel in the 5th–6th century, or perhaps even earlier. I present it here in the dated but still wonderful English rendition (from the age of Kipling) by Israel Zangwill, which itself has become a classic.

> All the world shall come to serve Thee
>   And bless Thy glorious name,
> And Thy righteousness triumphant
>   The islands shall acclaim.
> And the peoples shall go seeking
>   Who knew Thee not before,
> And the ends of earth shall praise Thee,
>   And tell Thy greatness o'er.
>
> They shall build for Thee their altars,
>   Their idols overthrown,
> And their graven gods shall shame them
>   As they turn to Thee alone.
> They shall worship Thee at sunrise
>   And feel Thy kingdom's might,
> And impart their understanding
>   To those astray in night.

> They shall testify Thy greatness,
>   And of Thy power speak,
> And extol Thee shrined, uplifted
>   Beyond man's highest peak.
> And with reverential homage,
>   Of love and wonder born,
> With the ruler's crown of beauty
>   Thy head they shall adorn.
> With the coming of Thy kingdom
>   The hills shall break into song,
> And the Islands laugh exultant
>   That they to God belong.
> And all their congregations
>   So loud Thy praise shall sing,
> That the uttermost peoples, hearing,
>   Shall hail Thee crowned King![18]

The sentiment of this poem is as grandly universalistic as we can find in the liturgy of early Judaism. It does not refer to Israel at all, but turns toward a vision of the future conversion of all peoples to worship of the single God, the universal Creator. It does retain a strong distinction between true and false religion ("idolatry"), but it sees the ultimate triumph of true faith as an exultant moment of conversion of spirit, rather than as an apocalyptic battle. There is no "conversion to Judaism" required of the nations in this "great day of the Lord," but only a joyous recognition that we humans are all one in recognizing God's kingship.

To offer a contrast to this universalist hymn, I will select from a medley of liturgical texts, all from the classic rabbinic period (2nd–4th century CE). There is not a single text I can think of

---

[18] Found in all traditional *maḥzorim* in the repetition of mussaf on the High Holy Days. This translation originally appeared in the old Adler maḥzor, but has been copied in many others as well.

that will give us full demonstration of this aspect of Jewish liturgy, but this grouping together will make the point.

From an introduction to the Rosh Hashanah Malkhuyot, later adopted for use as a concluding prayer for each daily service:

> It is our duty to praise the Lord of all
> To ascribe greatness to the Creator
> Who has not made us like the nations of [other] lands
> And not situated us like the peoples of the earth
> (For they bow down to vanity and emptiness
> And to a god who does not save)[19]
> But we kneel, bow, and offer gratitude
> To the King of kings, the blessed Holy One.

From the festival 'amidah:

> You have chosen us from among all peoples,
> You have loved and desired us.
> You have raised us up from among all other tongues
> And made us holy through Your commandments.

Regarding the Sabbath, from the Shabbat morning liturgy:

> You have not given it, O Y-H-W-H our God
> To the nations of the world.
> Nor have You granted it to those who worship idols,
> And the uncircumcised may not shelter in its rest.
> You gave it to Your people whom You love,
> The seed of Jacob whom You chose.

---

[19] Eliminated by censorship from the Ashkenazic version.

From the Havdalah service, concluding the Sabbath:

> Blessed are You Y-H-W-H our God, universal Ruler,
> Who distinguishes holy from profane, light from darkness.
> Israel from the nations,
> The seventh day from the six days of labor.
> Blessed are You Y-H-W-H, who distinguishes the holy from the profane.

Israel's special status as God's own and uniquely holy people, so clearly stated in these passages, is recognized throughout the liturgy and is essentially taken for granted as an axiom of the rabbinic tradition, supported by a wide array of biblical prooftexts. It is hard to argue that these texts do not indicate a degree of superiority over all the rest of the world's peoples. You have chosen us from among all others, *lifted us higher* than [those who speak] all other languages of the world. The contrast between Israel and the nations is like that between the holy and the profane, between light and darkness. Israel is chosen and beloved in a unique and exclusive manner. Yes, they are chosen to be God's *servants*, to fulfill their mission of bringing awareness of Y-H-W-H to all humanity. But that role itself is seen within the sources as the greatest possible human privilege.[20]

The midrash contains a well-known story that seems to reflect an early embarrassment about this notion of the election of Israel. According to the tale, God went to other nations first and offer them His Torah. The Ishmaelites rejected it when they heard that it included the prohibition against theft, presumably

---

[20] It should be noted that Mordecai Kaplan, in his *Reconstructionist Prayerbook* of 1945, already advocated deletion of all these passages. Some Reform liturgies since then, to one degree or another, have followed his lead.

because marauding and stealing was their very way of life. The descendants of Esau did the same when they heard that murder was prohibited, reflecting a similar reason. Only then did God turn to Israel, who said "We shall do, and we shall listen," putting their commitment to obey before they even heard further details of the commandments.[21]

Of course, this attempt at apologetics makes things even worse. Here we have an ancient Jewish stereotyping of the Arab as marauding thief and of the Roman (and afterwards, the Christian) as brutal murderer. These are carried through, in the later Jewish imagination, to shape views of Islam and Christendom. This is not to say that such stereotypes reflected nothing of reality. Indeed, we know well that stereotypes exist because they contain some grain of truth or memory of real and painful experience. But this also tells us how Jews were beginning to view the surrounding societies amid which they lived, quite early in our history.

The argument usually made in defense of these sources is that they were a response to the severe degradation and persecution that Jews experienced throughout the ages. They served as a counterpoint to the ongoing oppression of Jews, asserting that we were, in fact, superior, rather than inferior, sorts of humans, as the society around us seemed to insist. But that order of things needs to be called into question. These texts date from the 2nd–4th century. The oppression of Jews and the denunciation of Judaism were real both in the late Roman empire and in the era of early Christian hegemony. But this was long before the Crusades, the Black Death, and the truly awful demonization of the Jews that took place in the Middle Ages. To dismiss all this as Jewish response to suffering may be an easy way of getting ourselves "off the hook." We have to face fearlessly the possibility

---

[21] Mekhilta, ba-ḥodesh 5.

that our sense of superiority and condescension toward others was an early part of our tradition, perhaps one that even played some role in shaping the long and terrible history that we were to endure.

From a relatively early date, we Jews saw ourselves as God's faithful remnant, survivors of relentless persecution. We were God's innocent and precious flock, clinging tenaciously to our faith, calling out to God to save us from those who ever sought to destroy us, either by murder or by forced conversion. Another early anonymous poem, still recited each weekday in our morning prayers, tells the story best:

> Guardian of Israel! Protect our remnant!
> Let Israel not be cast away,
> Those who call out *Shema' Yisra'el* ("Hear O Israel")
> Each day.
>
> Guardian of this unique people!
> Let them not be cast away,
> Those who go on to say
> Y-H-W-H our God, Y-H-W-H is One!
> Each day.
>
> Guardian of this holy people!
> Let this holy folk not be cast away,
> Those who acclaim You
> As Holy! Holy! Holy!
> Each day.

One can hardly imagine how powerfully this ancient prayer resounded in the ears of those who survived each round of murderous persecutions that marked Jewish history through the ages, even more so for those who survived the Holocaust of the mid-20th century, about 1,500 years after it was written.

The Process of Internalization

Judaism in the Middle Ages (9th–15th centuries) saw itself as having already received the tradition in more or less fixed form. The Talmud was a sealed document and its commentators and summarizers were already active. The period of original creation of the tradition was at an end, and the essential contents of Jewish praxis were a received form that could be disputed only at the margins. The ongoing codification of praxis left it progressively more closed to debate. The question now became one of how to understand this received tradition, including both *halakhah* and *aggadah*, and how to interpret it in the light of the new intellectual and spiritual currents of the era.

We should recall that medieval Jewish intellectual history is divisible into two periods. From the 9th–12th centuries, most of the important creative efforts of Jewry took place in the context of Jews living as a minority within Muslim societies, ranging from the Near East all the way across North Africa into Spain. Often, but not always, these were relatively tolerant. In the later medieval era, from the 13th–15th centuries, the Christian setting dominated, including Christian Spain, France, and the Rhineland communities.

Medieval Jewish thinkers, even though representing significantly different schools of thought, had in common an understanding that the biblical/rabbinic tradition did not have to be taken only literally. The Torah's most important purpose was to teach the elements of proper faith and praxis, and these could be derived by a careful rereading of selected Torah verses. Philosophers and kabbalists had this notion in common. The differences between them had to do with the sources and methodologies of their reinterpretations of tradition, not with the legitimacy of that effort of ongoing reinterpretation itself. In that important sense, Judaism by nature is a "non-fundamentalist" tradition.

Although the process called *midrash* had already existed for many centuries, the Islamic world gave to Judaism a distinction between what it called exoteric and esoteric forms of exegesis. The notion of allowing for an esoteric reading of Sacred Writ was developed by Muslim scholars, who learned to read the Qur'an on a secret as well as revealed level. The outer meaning of the text, referred to in Hebrew as *nigleh*, remained close to the surface meaning of the words and verses before one. But there was also an inner meaning, called *nistar*, and that could be derived in various ways, depending upon one's intellectual framework. Some biblical interpreters went further, developing a fourfold way of reading Scripture. These included *peshat*, the direct interpretation of the text; *drash*, meaning the midrashic meanings offered to it in the rabbinic sources; *remez*, philosophical and allegorical readings; and *sod*, secret, the innermost reading of the text, following the new language of kabbalistic symbolism.

The point remained that the tradition was to be seen as cumulative. All that had been said in the past was affirmed as true; it just had to be given new meanings. And that was viewed as an entirely legitimate process. The era was characterized widely by a pursuit of deeper truth, a level of meaning in life as well as Scripture that was not immediately apparent to the casual eye. As religion and philosophy were drawn together in the medieval mind, their study was understood as an acquisition of wisdom, meant both as a personal quality and as an understanding of the ancient secrets of existence. The word ḥakham, or sage, took on a different meaning than that which it had in the rabbinic period. It no longer referred only to mastery of Jewish texts and traditions, but to a broader sense of what it meant to be a profoundly thinking or wise human being. The most open-minded Jewish teachers (more so in the Islamic setting) understood that there were such ḥakhamim outside the Jewish community, including both the ancient Greek and contemporary Muslim philosophers, and that they should be respected as such.

The first great work dedicated to an understanding of Judaism as an inward spiritual path was that called *Ḥovot ha-Levavot* or "Duties of the Hearts," written in 11th-century Spain by Baḥya Ibn Paquda. Originally composed in Arabic, its Hebrew translation was widely distributed and printed over the course of many centuries. It contained chapters on such matters as awe, trust, faith, and other aspects of the inward religious life. Baḥya praised the value of meditation in prayer, making it clear that this was something he had learned from Sufi practitioners in the surrounding culture. He speaks very highly of them as models of the serious and inward religious life and commends them for their personal piety.

While the medievals did not have a sense of the term "religion" as we understand it, they certainly spoke of both knowledge of God and devotion to God (*daʿat Y-H-W-H* and *ʿavodat Y-H-W-H*). They understood that these existed in all three of the religious communities that were known to them, although each certainly believed that the others were guilty of serious theological errors and hence were the "wrong" religions. The writings of medieval sages are filled with both direct and subtle attacks on the other traditions surrounding them and apologetic defenses of the religious tradition to which the author belonged. The Jews, being in the least fortuitous political situation, had the greatest need to be apologetic or defensive.

The turn toward a contemplative and introspective sort of Judaism that we find in Baḥya's masterpiece was both influential and representative of a trend that continued forward for many centuries. It influenced theologians and preachers as well as poets. A

Judaism centered on the life of inner religious devotion began to emerge both in Islam-dominated areas (Isaac of Accho and Avraham Maimuni are important examples) and in the newly growing communities along the Rhine, in the work of a group known to history as Ḥasidey Ashkenaz. Moses Maimonides himself, the greatest of Jewish philosophers of the era, was also a person of deep inward piety, as reflected throughout his writings. In him, the pursuit of philosophical truth and the pure life of piety were completely intertwined.

The rationalist tradition, which emerged in the 10th–12th centuries, understood that the universal God whom Judaism worshiped, the one Creator (He is often referred to as *ha-Bore'*, "Creator," in their writings) was also the God of the surrounding peoples. Devotion to this God, therefore, took on a certain universalistic character. Philosophic or metaphysical truth was one, transcending the borders between traditions. That being the case, Judaism is primarily distinguished from its daughter religions by its practice, the *halakhah*. This was emerging in codified fashion in the same generations, and sometimes even by the hands of the same people, as those writing works of speculative philosophy. It was therefore natural that they would consider this realm as central to defining Jewish life. When it came to the other branch of inherited rabbinic tradition, *aggadah*, there was much more ambiguity. Many of the tales, sayings, and especially the midrashic interpretations of scripture inherited from earlier generations, were causes of confusion and embarrassment to these rationalist generations. Both Muslim and Karaite scholars made mockery of the fanciful interpretations of the rabbis. There arose a significant tendency, including in the writings of Maimonides himself, to set aside difficult statements in the *aggadah* or to take them less than seriously.

A degree of tension inevitably began to arise between the philosophical claims and the devotional aspirations of Jewish thinkers in the high Middle Ages. While Neoplatonism certainly made room for the soul's longing for God or its return to the source of light, the abstractions seemingly demanded by philosophic rigor brought forth a God-idea that was far from being the one of warm personal relationship that been familiar in earlier forms of Judaism. God became for the philosophers precisely that, an idea. In order to "purify" that idea, one had to deny anything that might seem anthropomorphic, or even explain away any passage in scripture attributing *emotion*, or feeling, to God, a characteristic that seemed to belong to humans alone. Medieval thinkers were aware of the element of projection that lay in all human understandings of the divine, and they sought to get beyond it by insistence on demonstrable philosophic truth.

But it was not only the personal devotional needs of Israelites that lay unfulfilled by rational thinking about matters of religion. The historical situation of the Jews, seeing themselves as now in exile for 1,000 years, required explanation, or at least a sympathetic ear. Philosophy tends to live in the upper realms, more interested in the movement of the spheres than in history, including the exile and suffering of those who had thought they were God's chosen people. The Jewish people and its place in the world had been a major subject of thought in the rabbinic era. Israel was the people for whom God had created the world. It was the righteous among Israel who preserved the world's existence. "Wherever Israel were exiled, the *shekhinah*, divine presence, was exiled with them."[22] Philosophy, arising in the more cosmopolitan atmosphere of the Middle Ages, tended to ignore this very particularistic reality.

Thus, a significant gap began to arise between religious thinkers of the age and the community that they were said to lead. The folk spirit remained much closer to the God of the old biblical and rabbinic tradition, the one reflected in the texts that most

---

[22] Megillah 29a, and frequently.

people knew best, the Torah and the prayerbook. Jews were looking toward a God who would lessen their suffering and redeem them from exile. They needed an explanation of why they had both survived and suffered among the nations and what remained of their mission in a world so dominated by other faiths. The pursuit of philosophy was not likely to bring answers to these existential questions.

Into this gap stepped a poet and philosopher called Yehudah Halevi (1075–1141). Well educated and refined in ways that reflected the very height of Spanish Jewry in the Golden Age, Halevi, already in his youth, composed poetry that made a deep impression. His poetic oeuvre was wide-ranging, including both secular and religious poems, a good deal of love poetry, and much more. He is best known, however, for poetry expressing Jewish national longings, including a great attachment to the Land of Israel and the dream of both past and future Jewish life and glory there.

A millennium of exile and wandering had not dampened the Jewish sense that one day our exiles would be ingathered and restored to the Holy Land. This would be initiated by Messiah and would bring about a glorious age of national rebirth and renewal. Within this messianic belief, no clear distinction was made between the redemption of the Jews and the transformation of all reality, including that of the natural world, into an ideal state. Somehow, they would all come about together. The redemption of Israel was to serve as a paradigm for universal deliverance, the exile of Israel from Jerusalem serving as a microcosmic reflection of the exile of all humanity from Eden. National and universal redemption were two faces of the same dream.

The poet produced a theological treatise known as the *Kuzari*.[23] It was composed in the form of a dramatic dialogue between the

---

[23] Available in several English translations, but beware of apologetics.

pagan king of the Khazars and the rabbi who came to teach him in the course of his decision to convert himself and his people to Judaism. This setting was based on a real historical event, the embrace of Judaism by the Khazars (a tribe in what is now southern Ukraine) in the 9th or 10th century. Halevi uses it for what may be called both a defense of Judaism and a Jewish theological attack on the enterprise of rational philosophy itself. True religion, he claims, must be based on revelation, rather than on rational discourse. Each of the three traditions—Judaism, Christianity, and Islam—makes a claim to such revelation of the word of God. The other two, of course, are further developments of the original revelation to Israel at Mount Sinai. That revelation alone, however, was witnessed by an entire people, one transformed forever by the impact of that event. The power of that revelation has never been superseded, despite the claims of Judaism's two daughter religions.

While the revelation of Sinai has universal implications, it was given in a very specific way to a particular people. God chose this people to be the receivers and historic bearers of His word because of a special quality that they bore. Here Halevi turns to medieval theories that claimed particular characteristics for each nation and its geographical setting. Each of the nations of the world is blessed with unique characteristics, making it appropriate that they were settled in their particular lands. The Creator saw that Israel had a particular talent for what Halevi names "the spiritual matter" and that the holy Land of Israel was the proper place for its spiritual enterprise to be realized, through prophecy. Hence there is a particular bond between God (who is both the universal Creator and the One who has elected Israel), the Jewish people, and the Land. While this bond has been suspended for many centuries, due to the sins of ancient Israel, it has never been broken and Judaism is sustained by hope for its renewal.

Here, the promise of the Land is precisely linked to the uniquely holy character of the Jew as a special sort of human being. For Halevi, this specialness is still very much about *service* of God. There is nothing in it that is about lording over others. Jews were simply capable, because of this special talent, to understand how to serve God more fully, and could do so best in their Holy Land. It may be that Halevi himself did not recognize the chauvinistic implications of this idea. The Jews in his day, after all, were a scattered and helpless people. It should also be noted that Halevi personally attested to his longing for the Land of Israel by journeying there toward the end of his life. He died either in Jerusalem, which was then under Crusader rule, or on the way to it. Widespread legend has long assumed that he died a martyr's death.

The romantic theology of the *Kuzari* was an ideological framing for emotions that Halevi expressed most powerfully in some of his poetry. The wonderful Hebrew poetry of 10th- to 12th-century Spain had an incredibly wide range, including both secular and religious themes. The religious poetry was filled with praise for Creation, the soul's love of God, and Israel's longing for redemption. To illustrate the spirit of the age, I select two poems, one by Halevi himself and the other by his near-contemporary, Solomon Ibn Gabirol. The former, "God, to Whom Shall I Compare Thee?" again reflects the universal face of Judaism in its era. Here, in contrast to Halevi's *Kuzari*, his religious vision shows a universal embrace. While it has a liturgical setting (an introduction to the *Kedushah*, parallel to the *Sanctus* in Christian liturgy), it is the call of a religious soul beholding the universe and its wonders, stretching far beyond any boundaries of nation or tradition. Again, the translation is by Israel Zangwill. These Victorian translations, I find, best reflect the rhyming and the antiquity of language encountered in the Hebrew originals.

GOD, WHOM SHALL I COMPARE TO THEE?[24]

Yehuda Halevi

God! whom shall I compare to Thee,
    When Thou to none canst likened be?
    Under what image shall I dare
    To picture Thee, when ev'rywhere
    All Nature's forms Thine impress bear?
Greater, O Lord! Thy glories are
    Than all the heavenly chariot far.
    Whose mind can grasp Thy world's design?
    Whose word can fitly Thee define?
    Whose tongue set forth Thy powers divine?
Can heart approach, can eye behold
    Thee in Thy righteousness untold?
    Whom didst Thou to Thy counsel call,
    When there was none to speak withal
    Since Thou wast first and Lord of all?
Thy world eternal witness bears
    That none its Maker's glory shares.
    Thy wisdom is made manifest
    In all things formed by Thy behest,
    All with Thy seal's clear mark imprest.
Before the pillars of the sky
    Were raised, before the mountains high
    Were wrought, ere hills and dales were known,
    Thou in Thy majesty alone
    Didst sit, O God! upon Thy throne!
Hearts, seeking Thee, from search refrain,
    And weary tongues their praise restrain.

---

[24] The Hebrew original is to be found in Hayyim Schirmann's *Ha-Shirah ha-'Ivrit bi-Sefarad uve-Provens* (Dvir, 1961), v. 2, 532-536.

> Thyself unbound by time and place,
> Thou dost pervade, support, embrace
> The world and all created space.
> The sages' minds bewildered grow,
> The lightning-speed of thought is slow.
> "Awful in praises" art Thou named;
> Thou fillest, strong in strength proclaimed,
> This universe Thy hand has framed.
> Deep, deep beyond all fathoming,
> Far, far beyond all measuring,
> We can but seek Thy deeds alone;
> When bow Thy saints before Thy throne
> Then is Thy faithfulness made known.
> Thy righteousness we can discern,
> Thy holy law proclaim and learn.
> Is not Thy presence near alway
> To them who penitently pray,
> But far from those who sinning stray?
> Pure souls behold Thee, and no need
> Have they of light: they hear and heed
> Thee with the mind's keen ear, although
> The ear of flesh be dull and slow.
> Their voices answer to and fro.
> Thy holiness forever they proclaim:
> The Lord of Hosts! Thrice holy is Thy name!

The poem is notable for its utter universality. What we hear in it is the voice of a religious human being, not necessarily that of a Jew. The wonders of nature, the longing of the soul, the quest for wisdom are all themes found throughout medieval Western religion, well transcending the borders of particularity.

The second poem (a particular favorite of mine because of its later echo in a story of S. Y. Agnon) is a lament over the fate of

Israel and an outcry to God to end her bitter exile. Gabirol's cry echoes that of Israel's ancient prophets, to whom he was a worthy heir. The poem is rife with both pain and hope, but the powerful refrain is a call, perhaps even a challenge, to God, to change Israel's fate. The poem was probably not composed as liturgy, but it was recited for some time as a (now neglected) part of the Ashkenazic rite. The translation is by Nina Salomon, but with some emendations.

CAPTIVE OF SORROW[25]
Solomon Ibn Gabirol

Captive of sorrow on a foreign shore,
A handmaid as in Egypt's slavery:
Through the dark days of bereavement sore
She looketh only unto Thee.
Restore her sons, O Mighty One of old!
Her remnant tenth shall cause man's strife to cease.
O speed the message, swiftly be she told
Good tidings, which Elijah shall unfold:
Daughter of Zion, sing aloud! Behold
Thy prince of peace!

How long, O Lord, 'til when
Will You neglect us yet again?

Surely a limit boundeth every woe,
But my enduring anguish hath no end;
My grievous years are spent in ceaseless flow,
My wound hath no amend.
O'erwhelmed, my helm doth fail, no hand is strong
Enough to steer to port, her longed-for aim.

---
[25] Schirmann v. 1, 247-249.

How long, O Lord, wilt thou my doom prolong?
When shall be heard the dove's sweet voice of song?
O leave us not to perish for our wrong,
We who in good faith bear Thy name.

How long, O Lord, 'til when
Will You neglect us yet again?

Wounded and crushed, beneath my load I sigh,
Despised, abject, outcast, and trampled low;
How long, O Lord, shall I of violence cry,
My heart dissolve with woe?
How many years, without a gleam of light
Has suffering been our lot, our portion pain!
With Ishmael as a lion in his might
And Esau an owl of darkest night.
Beset from side to side, behold our plight
Betwixt the twain.

How long, O Lord, 'til when
Will You neglect us yet again?

Is this Thy voice,
The call of captive Ariel's woe now healed?
Virgin of Israel, arise, rejoice!
In Daniel's vision, lo, the end is sealed.
When Michael from the height
Shall stand aloft in strength,
And shout aloud in might:
Our redeemer's come at length!
Amen, amen, behold
The Lord's decree foretold.
As Thou hast our souls afflicted sore

> Wilt Thou make us glad forevermore!
>
> How long, O Lord, 'til when
> Will You neglect us yet again?

"Ishmael" and "Esau" in the poem refer to the Islamic and Christian realms. The author, a Jew living in Spain, feels like a bit of small prey, perhaps a dove, caught between them, the lion and the owl.

In sharp contrast to Halevi, Moses Maimonides (writing a half century later) was quite cautious regarding the chosen status of the Jewish people. He makes virtually no mention of it in his *Guide to the Perplexed*, apparently because he did not consider it to be a philosophically defensible claim. While far from denying such a pillar of rabbinic teaching, he was careful always to present it in the context of universal good. God had chosen the Jews in order to make His truth known to the world. That choice begins with Abraham, a seeker who turned to God in a process of religious self-discovery. It was the example of Abraham that set the tone for Maimonides' concept of the ideal relationship between God and the seeker, most fully exemplified in Moses. The revelation of Sinai was essentially a "meeting of the minds" between the divine intellect and that of an individual who had prepared himself properly (both philosophically and morally), rather than a public display to the entire people.

It will be no great surprise to learn that Halevi's romanticism triumphed over the greater philosopher's hesitation. We need to think only of the better recalled European romantic movement in the 19th century that swept away the brief era of Enlightenment rationalism and liberalism that had come before it, bringing nationalism in its wake. The popularity and ultimate vindication of ideas has more to do than we like to admit with deep inner feelings and needs of a broader population, those who live outside the ivory tower. The vigor of religion lies in its ability to both articulate and respond to those needs. Jewish thought in the 13th century was dominated by a strong anti-Maimonidean reaction, one that sought to recapture some of the religious passion that had been lost amid the careful calculation of what one may or may not say about God as a matter of philosophical truth.

The importance of Jewish separateness and the conscious effort to keep us apart from others was reflected in the development of medieval *halakhah* as well, particularly as the center shifted toward Ashkenaz. Such restrictions as those that govern sharing wine with Gentiles, eating bread or cooked foods prepared by them, and any imitation of gentile customs, evidence this concern.

Kabbalah, a Judaism of Myth and Symbol

This reaction emerged within circles that understood Judaism indeed as a way of serving God, indeed a *derekh* in *'avodah*. For Jews, it was the only proper way of life. Anyone who transgressed it was considered a sinner, violating the great privilege of having been born an Israelite. The ancient notion that it was only Israel's worship that sustained the universe, that Israel was God's "first-born son" (Ex. 4:22), persisted in the folk imagination and was given intellectual articulation in this new round of anti-rationalist writings. While Maimonides and other rationalists had understood that both Muslims and Christians worshipped the same God as did the Jews, there persisted in these circles a sense that it was only the worship of Israel that really mattered.

Within the writings of those anti-rationalist writers, mostly Bible commentators and preachers, we begin to see evidence of a new religious language starting to emerge. Rather than trying to talk about God in philosophical terms, an old-new set of symbols is being used to allow for discourse on a different, more profoundly esoteric and spiritually evocative level. These symbols are drawn from a variety of sources, including the natural world, the Torah text, and the realm of Jewish religious practice. They have an ancient and authentic sounding Jewish ring to them, and yet they are being used in an entirely new way. This is the language of Kabbalah, a world of Jewish mystical teaching that first appears in documents of this era.

The earliest origins of this symbolic language are themselves shrouded in mystery, one much discussed by scholars in our day. An especially obscure book called *Bahir* (Clarity), partially written somewhere in the Near East but re-edited in southern France, is the earliest source we have for this new sort of religious discourse. But by the mid-13th century it is being used by a wide range of authors in Provence, Catalonia, and Castile. Notably, these are all areas of Christian domination, where the hostility toward Jews and Judaism was much greater than in the Andalusian culture of Muslim Spain (yes, there are some exceptions in both directions). It may well be that the insecurity caused by this greater hostility helped to call forth a deeper assertion of Judaism's exclusive truth, a reaction of the literal demonization of Jews in the surrounding culture.

This symbolic language came to be known as Kabbalah. Literally, the word means "the received" or "tradition," likely a cover for what was in fact a radically innovative way of thinking. Kabbalah created within Judaism a metaphysical understanding of the universe, its origins, and its ongoing structure, based on myth and symbol, rather than on intellectual proposition. It was forever pasting together fragments of philosophy that suited its purpose (often from neo-Platonic sources) with snippets of biblical text and old rabbinic *aggadah*. For those open to it and understanding its secrets, it addressed the heart in a particularly profound way. Both the Torah text and daily religious life took a new meaning for those who understood them as embodying Kabbalistic truth. It made particularly strong use of those very passages in scripture and *aggadah* from which the philosophers had tended to shy away. These became, in many cases, the embodiments of Torah's most esoteric teachings.

In characterizing this literature as mystical, we mean to say that it seeks to explore the link between the origins and meaning of the universe and the inner experiential world of the seekers themselves. The human soul is a microcosm; in it one can discover the secrets of the universe. Found across the many religious traditions of the world, mystics proclaim an underlying oneness of being that can be attained, or at least glimpsed, by the inward journey of the devotee. All of the symbolic language and forms of religion exist in order to stimulate that journey, to bring the mystic into an intimate encounter with the divine source, and to allow the mind to return to this world, enriched by the journey rather than destroyed by it.

Kabbalah begins with an accounting of how multiplicity first originated from within the oneness of God. All that exists is an emanating flow from within that secret oneness, never fully separated from it. "Creation" is thus understood as a self-manifestation of the hidden One. The ten stages in that outflowing process also make up the tenfold structure of Kabbalah's symbolic language. Together, these ten constitute an inner divine universe, one in which dynamic interaction among these stages, each represented by a wide array of symbols, reveals a dramatic and ever-changing picture of the inner life of God.

This self-manifesting process of God in Creation is repeated in the revelation of Torah to Moses and Israel at Mount Sinai, and through the ongoing divinely guided process of interpretation. Here the revelation is verbal, ensconced in words and letters rather than in the creatures of the natural world. Because of the parallel between these two forms of divine self-revelation, the Torah text serves as a guide to the worlds both above and within the soul. Study of Torah and fulfillment of the *mitzvot*, always the central virtues and obligations within Judaism, are now understood as a path of ascent into the divine realm and a way of bringing its blessings down to earth.

The human being, in bodily form as well as in soul, is created in the divine image. Here this means that the inward structure of the self is parallel to that of the cosmos. Ultimate self-exploration therefore leads one to knowing God. Human mental and emotional states reflect the *sefirot*, the inner divine stages. If maintained in purity, they may serve as "thrones" upon which these aspects of divinity come to alight, thus becoming manifest in the world.

All of this teaching is presented by the kabbalists not as an abstract doctrine but by way of interpreting scripture and other ancient Jewish writings. It is deeply integrated with the language and emotional content of prior tradition. In contrast to philosophy, it sought to hide any elements of non-Jewish influence that might be found within it. Kabbalah presented itself as the language of the Jewish soul, something unique to this much maligned and underestimated tradition. It spoke fully and compassionately of the sufferings of Israel, depicting the feminized *shekhinah* or divine presence as wandering through their exile at their side, sharing in their woe.

Not surprisingly, a good deal of speculation is found in the *Zohar*, the most important document of classical Kabbalah, and elsewhere about the nature of the soul itself. What is the source of the human soul and how does it come to reflect the world above? Much of this talk is centered around the tripartite division of the soul under the names *nefesh, ruaḥ,* and *neshamah*. While one might literally translate these as "self, spirit, and breath," that does not tell us very much. All of them are biblical terms, and the three parts are well documented in the older sources. As it happens, the Greco-Arabic philosophy current in the Middle Ages also believed in three parts of the soul, and there is much discussion in the Jewish sources seeking to coordinate the rabbinic and philosophic traditions.

The soul, particularly *neshamah*, represents the divine presence within the human being. As we saw above, it is the result of God's blowing the breath of life into each human, repeating the original gift to Adam. There are some passages in rabbinic sources that depict "soul" in a somewhat abstract manner. "Just as God fills all the world, so does the soul fill the entire body."[26] But the soul is mostly seen as an actual substance, one that enters the body at conception or at birth and departs at the hour of one's death. In later Kabbalistic writings, we frequently encounter the phrase "the soul is a part of God above."[27]

The question we have to ask is whether this applies to all souls or only the souls of Israel. The inner logic of the concept, one might say, is of course universal. Adam's soul contains within it the souls of all his descendants, every human who is ever to be born. As we are all in God's image, so do we all bear divine souls. Souls may be divided into righteous and wicked, into pure and blemished, but there should logically not be any difference on the level of soul between Jews and non-Jews.

But that is by no means the way things are usually depicted. We find repeatedly, especially in the later mystical sources, that all the souls *of Israel* were present in Adam. How can that be? What about all the rest of human souls? It turns out (more as taken for granted than as clearly stated) that the only souls that are truly contained in the Adamic "body"—which exists until the end of time—are the legitimate souls brought into the world through the union of Adam and Eve. They are the souls that result from the sublime pairing of "male" and "female" within the divine sphere, the holy union of the blessed Holy One and *shekhinah*, the feminized Divine Presence.

These are the souls of Israel. There are, of course, speculations regarding the origin of the other souls, those of "the nations," the seventy peoples of the world. Sometimes they are said to be conceived from within the *kelipot*, the pernicious "shells" or "husks" that hide the light of divinity. In some sources, they are said to result from the illicit union of Adam with Lilith, Eve's demonic

---

[26] Berakhot 10a.
[27] First found in *Shefa' Tal* by R. Shabtai Sheftel Horowitz (1561-1619).

twin. Or they are descended from Cain, rather than from Seth, the father of true humanity.[28] In the Kabbalistic tradition absorbed by some schools within Hasidism, non-Jews are devoid of the divine *neshamah* altogether, possessing only the lowest portion of the soul, that which keeps one alive.

As is the case throughout Judaism, there is room for many opinions about such matters. Even within the mystical sources, there is variation in the degree and extremity with which these views were held. Account had to be taken, to be sure, for the souls of future proselytes and for those who were to be designated as the "righteous among the nations." There is much discussion, especially of the convert's soul, in the *Zohar*. Perhaps these, some sources suggest, might have been born from that less dense level of "shell" where some degree of light shines through, called *kelipat nogah*. Exposure to the light of Torah will help to awaken deeply hidden sparks of light from within their souls.

What happens within Kabbalah in general is a revival of ancient tropes of mythic consciousness, stemming from a collective memory within the people that had never quite been vanquished. The pain of Judea's defeat, the Temple's destruction, and the sufferings of exile stirred a brewing hostility to the outside world, that of "the wicked kingdom" that continued to endure and rule. While Jewish philosophers had depicted a Judaism that was far from these mythic undercurrents, the much more popular ongoing fantasy world of later midrashic writings sustained them and developed them further.

With regard to the souls of the nations, what we see is the coming together of the special status of Jews as God's chosen people, abundant in the biblical and rabbinic sources, and Yehudah Halevi's notion (though perhaps not exclusively his) that Jews possess a particular faculty for attaining spiritual insight.

---

[28] Tikkuney Zohar 69, 117a-118a.

That special faculty came to be identified with the divine element within the soul itself, the part of the human being capable of rising to become one with God, or to bring blessing into the world.

There are even sources that describe Jews as an entirely different sort of creature than others. God's creations, in the terminology of medieval Hebrew, are divided among *domem*, the inanimate; *tsomeah*, the vegetative; *hai*, the animal; and *medabber*, the human (literally, "the speaker"). But some then add another category: *yisra'el*, the Jew, something of a super-human, a species all its own. This is the influence of the *Kuzari*, translated into abstract categories, but making a very concrete statement.

The influence of Kabbalah increased greatly in the 16th century, following the expulsion of the Jews from the Iberian peninsula. The Sephardic diaspora spread across the Mediterranean, largely into lands dominated by the Ottoman empire. In that culture, members of each religious community had significant independence with regard to legal, educational, and other matters, in addition to the practice of religion itself. The so-called *millet* system left each tradition to proclaim its own exclusive truth. So long as it brought about no clash with members of other communities, especially the dominant Muslims, the government did not intervene. The belief of each group in the unique superiority of its own religious claims was taken for granted. Jews in the Ottoman world lived a significantly more separate existence from the surrounding culture than they had in Spain or Portugal. For the first time, they spoke a different language than those around them. Their culture was created entirely in Hebrew and Ladino.

At about the same time, the large migration eastward of Ashkenazi Jews began to take place. As various rulers in the principalities that constituted the future Germany exerted more pressure on Jewish life than could be tolerated, large numbers migrated, first to Bohemia and western Poland, but eventually eastward to the area now known as Lithuania, Belarus, and Ukraine. By the end of the 16th century, this part of Eastern Europe, the old Polish kingdom, and the Ottoman empire contained the great bulk of world Jewry. That remained the case until the end of the 19th century. In eastern Europe, as well, the Jews lived socially, linguistically, and culturally, as well as religiously, an existence quite totally separate from that of the surrounding population.

These were both settings in which the influence of Kabbalah spread quite undisturbed, both among the intelligentsia and the folk. The mid 16th century, some 50 years after the Spanish expulsion, saw the emergence of a new creative center in the Galilee town of Safed. This was a gathering of spiritual figures and intellectuals from various parts of the Ottoman diaspora. While the Safed community included leading figures in Jewish law as well as poets and preachers, the spiritual setting in which it all took place was a renewal of Kabbalah, proclaimed by Safed's emissaries and by the many works composed there as the new dominant ideology of Judaism. Both the story of this new gathering of sages in the Holy Land and the content of their teachings had great influence on Jewish communities throughout the world. Over the course of the ensuing century, every smallest detail in the daily life of Jewish observance was given profound esoteric significance in language derived from the teachings of Safed's kabbalists. Every word in the liturgy had a specific "address" toward which it was to turn its healing power, as the Jews were reconceived as the unique healers of a broken universe. Manuscripts of these teachings were sent and copied with great enthusiasm throughout the Jewish world.

Kabbalah needs to be understood as a cultural aura as a well as a specific set of teachings. The actual metaphysics taught by the disciples of Rabbis Moshe Cordovero and Isaac Luria were abstruse and complex. Surely only a small part of the population had the knowledge and acumen to even approach an understanding of them. As the generations went on, new interpreters added ever more layers of complexity to this newly received tradition. But the society was permeated with the sense that there existed a secret meaning to everything within the tradition, and that reinforced an aura of urgency in its fulfillment, even in those who made no claim to themselves understand the secrets.

There also existed a vast realm that was known as practical Kabbalah. This meant the knowledge and use of holy names and secret formulae for purposes of healing from illness and improving one's personal situation in various ways, the "bringing down" of divine blessing. This is an area that had always existed within Judaism, one that dwelt in the border realm between mysticism and magic. Now bits of ancient magical lore, fragmentarily preserved over many centuries, were joined to kabbalistic understandings of secret names of God and practices derived from the Safed teachers themselves. There was no clear border between the theoretical and practical aspects of the mystical tradition; many of the same people who studied profound mystical treatises also partook in, and some even made a living from, fulfilling the needs of simple people who came to them for such blessing.

Our two poems for this chapter are both creations of the Safed revival in the late 16th century. Each is an exquisite example of the rich life of piety created in that community. The first, *Yedid Nefesh*, was written by Rabbi Eleazar Azikri. He also authored a book of pious teachings, *Sefer Ḥaredim*, perhaps best translated as *The Book of the Quakers* (not referring, of course, to the Christian sect of that name). Although it makes no mention of *Shabbat*, it is now widely sung at the opening of the Shabbat evening service. The other was composed by the most famous kabbalist of Safed, Rabbi Isaac Luria. It was written for singing at the concluding meal of the Sabbath, a moment when a special intimacy is felt between the kabbalist and the aura of divine presence, combined with a sweet sadness at the Sabbath's approaching end.

SOUL'S BELOVED[29]
Rabbi Eleazar Azikri

Soul's beloved, merciful father,
   draw your servant to your will;
he'll run to you like a gazelle
   and bow before your splendor—
      for your love to him is sweeter
   than a taste of the honeycomb's nectar.

Majestic, magnificent world's luster,
   my soul is faint with love for you;
Heal her, O Lord, I beseech you,
   show her your brilliance's pleasure—
      then she will be strengthened and healed
   and serve your will forever.

Ancient of Days, may your mercies stir,
   take pity on him who loves you;
for long now has he yearned for you
   to see the glory of your power—
      Hasten, Lord, my heart's delight,
   do not ignore my desire.

Make yourself known, my spirit's treasure,
   spread the shelter of your peace about me;
let the world shine with your glory,
   in you then we will rejoice—
      Hurry, my beloved, the hour has come,
   be gracious as once you were.

---

[29] Translation by Peter Cole. From *The Poetry of Kabbalah: Mystical Verse from the Jewish Tradition*, translated, edited, and introduced by Peter Cole (Yale University Press, 2012), copyright © Peter Cole.

This reads like a purely private song of an individual's love and longing for God. Note especially the interweaving of images: God is the beloved, father, healer, and light. In style, it is reminiscent of religious love poetry one might find in the Sufi corpus. Safed, indeed, is close to Damascus, a major Sufi center, and there was a strong Sufi presence throughout the region. Only in the poem's final line does *ve-hannenu* ("be gracious" *to us*) imply a sense of specific Jewish context. The Luria poem that follows is quite different in that way.

SONS OF THE PALACE[30]
Rabbi Isaac Luria

Sons of the Palace—
   you who yearn
to behold the radiance
   of the Lesser Presence—

be seated here
   at this Sabbath table,
adorned and crowned
   with the Name of the King.

Exult in your being
   part of this gathering
among the guardian
   angels' wings,

and rejoice now
   within this hour

---

[30] Translation by Peter Cole. From *The Poetry of Kabbalah: Mystical Verse from the Jewish Tradition*, translated, edited, and introduced by Peter Cole (Yale University Press, 2012), copyright © Peter Cole.

of favor which knows
    not what anger brings.

Draw near me here—
    see my power,
without the judgments
    of judgment's terror.

Those without
    may not enter,
for they are dogs
    of rancor and gall.

I hereby call
    to the Ancient of Days
to summon His will
    to drive them away—

for when His favor
    in this room is shown,
the husks are rendered
    null and void.

He drives them into
    holes in the ground,
conceals them deep
    in caverns of stone.

And so it is
    now and till twilight—
within the Impatient
    One's delight.

The image of Israel as "Sons (or 'Children') of the Palace" is an ancient one, found in countless parables used throughout midrashic and later literature.[31] Our "palace" is the House of God, the Temple both above and below, from which we have been sent away and to which we long to return. Israel are the beloved and exiled child of the King.

The *kalbin de-ḥatsifin*, "dogs of rancor and gall" who may not enter this sacred assembly, are the evil spirits in their primary designation, but can also be taken to include non-Jews, whose souls are earthly incarnations of such spirits. At least, that is how the phrase was understood by one of the most important Hasidic masters, as we shall see below.

In the Mediterranean world, and particularly in North Africa, this kabbalistic culture flourished for several hundred years. The presence of a kabbalist within the community was considered a great, even necessary, asset. Visits to the graves of kabbalistic teachers from prior generations were also considered a great source of blessing. In central and Eastern Europe, there developed a particular sort of practitioner of practical Kabbalah known as a *ba'al shem*, literally "master of the name." These were essentially wandering folk healers, using their knowledge of secret names (and herbal medicines from the forest, to be sure) in areas where no glimmer of more scientific sorts of healing had yet appeared. In Poland and Ukraine too, the cultural dominance of a mystical spirit, including a belief in demons and other aspects of the popular religious imagination, grew strong, even among those who had little understanding of the kabbalistic teachings.

In this stage of our development, we see that chosenness, with its implications of superiority, and the conscious effort to keep us apart from others, have morphed into a fear-based demoni-

---

[31] It may be based on the Talmudic saying, widely quoted, that "All Israel are the Children of Kings," found in Shabbat 67a. The original context there has an entirely different meaning.

zation of those outside the covenant of Israel. It is likely that the kabbalistic sources are *reflecting* the cumulative embitterment of the Jews toward those who surrounded and oppressed them, as much as they were helping to create it.

From Kabbalah to Hasidism

Eastern European Hasidism represents one of the great success stories in the world history of religious movements. When Israel Ba'al Shem Tov, the figure around whose image the movement was to coalesce, died in 1760, there were no more than 20 or 30 people closely linked with him whom we could identify as laying claim to his legacy. All these were within Podolia, a somewhat remote corner of southeastern Poland, up against the Russian and Turkish borders. We have little knowledge of any influence he had beyond this group and his own town of Miedzhybosh.[32] Half a century later, ever larger swaths of eastern European Jewry, soon to become majorities in some areas, considered themselves followers of the movement that carried his banner and proclaimed his truth.

Hasidism may be seen as the transfer of the kabbalistic ethos from a small society of scholarly and retreating mystics to the creation of a popular movement of religious renewal based on their teachings. This demanded a radical simplification of kabbalistic doctrine and a highly selective reading of its sources. The movement was largely created by a remarkable group of revivalist preachers, who learned to mine the entire tradition, from biblical verses all the way up to latter-day mystical formulations, in ways that would rouse their hearers to a renewed sense of devotion and religious excitement. *Hitlahavut*, as they called it, meant becoming enflamed with the love of God.

The Ba'al Shem Tov himself was a remarkable figure. He seems

---

[32] There are tales in *Shivḥey ha-BeSHT* of the Ba'al Shem Tov traveling as far as Lithuania, but these cannot be confirmed.

to have come from the margins of Jewish society, and yet to have been accepted in his community with the status of "kabbalist in residence." According to legend, which in this case seems to make sense, he spent 10 years as a wandering semi-hermit in the Carpathian mountains, where he seems to have gained a great appreciation of the presence of God throughout Creation (what we would call "nature"). We do not know with whom he might have come into contact during those years of wandering. Recent scholarship suggests that this primitive area was filled with hermitlike monks from both the Ukrainian and Moldavian sides of those mountains, as well as bearers of Sufi, and perhaps other, more ancient, traditions. He earned his livelihood as a *ba'al shem*, one of those faith healers mentioned above. This is a level of traditional society where the borders between Jews and non-Jews and the various herbal recipes they might have to offer were least carefully guarded. Thus, the possibility of non-Jewish influences on his teachings cannot be dismissed lightly. These years of his early life also gave him an appreciation of simple folk, those who lived in such places, and the wisdom they might have to offer.

When he settled in the very respectable Jewish community of Miedzhybosh, sometime in the 1740s, people were originally suspect of him. A *ba'al shem* was seen as a potentially shady character, one who might have truck with evil spirits, aiding him in his work. But the BeSHT (as he is called) proved himself as teacher, rather than just healer, largely through his ability to respond to quotations of traditional text that were presented to him, always in novel and spiritually exciting ways. These quotations and his interpretations of them are preserved in the books of his disciples (he himself did not write) and form the earliest basis of Hasidic teachings. The BeSHT was also a fine storyteller. His use of parables, taken from daily life, did much to make his thoughts accessible.

In order to understand Hasidism, which I have been studying

and teaching for well over half a century, we need to outline some of the basic teachings it sought to offer. These articulations, distilled from the kabbalistic legacy, come from the movement's earliest period. They were to be reshaped significantly in the course of history, as we shall see; but the movement, even as it exists today, still bears something of the stamp of its founding generations. This means that it includes some of the most beautiful and also some of the most dangerous religious teachings to be found in the long history of Judaism:

1. God's presence (*shekhinah*) underlies, fills, and includes all of existence. There is no place, moment, or event that is not filled to the brim with divinity. Sparks of divine light are therefore to be found everywhere. The Jew's task is to seek out and discover those sparks, even in the seemingly most unlikely places, in order to raise them up, bring joy to *shekhinah*, and thus reestablish the divine unity that embraces all of being in oneness.

2. The purpose of life is the joyful service of God. God created the world in order to derive pleasure from the devotion of human beings, specifically from the souls of Israel. Our task is to provide that pleasure through constant good works and joyful praise. Be careful of anything that might keep you from that task, especially of excessive religious guilt or calls for self-punishment due to sin. These will only lead you astray from your single task of serving God in joy.

3. "God needs to be served in every way." It is not only through Torah study, prayer, and fulfilling specific commandments that we worship God. All of life, including the fulfillment of our physical needs, is to become an avenue of devotion. Transform and uplift every act you do and make it an act of worship.

4. The essence of religious life lies in inwardness and spiritual intensity. The great battle to be fought is that against

"learned" or routinized religious behavior, the opposite of spiritual enthusiasm. Outer deeds are important and the commandments are to be fulfilled in every detail, but they are to be seen as means rather than ends, as vessels for the divine light that floods the soul or as concrete embodiments of the heart's inward devotion. Even where the halakhic tradition says that a *mitzvah* may be fulfilled with the inward direction called *kavvanah*, the Hasidic teachings require it. "A *mitzvah* without *kavvanah* is like a body without a soul."

5. Our human task is that of uplifting and transforming our moral and emotional selves to become ever more perfect vehicles for God's service. This process begins with the key devotional pair of love and fear. We need to purify these in our lives, coming to realize that the only true love is the love of God and the only worthy fear is that of awe at standing in God's presence. All other loves and fears derive from these, but they come to us in a "fallen" state. True love and awe, and other emotions that follow them, become open channels through which God's blessing can flow into us.

It is not hard to identify a strong romantic sense in the religion being presented here. Kabbalah has been stripped of much of its esotericism and recast as a spiritual path accessible to both individual and community. The centering is entirely upon the inner life of the individual and the transformation of self and of perception. The traditional emphasis on learning, so characteristic of Judaism throughout the ages, has been significantly diminished. You do not need to be a scholar to serve God with all your heart. (This is why the rabbinate was originally so fiercely opposed to Hasidism.) While the theosophical teachings of earlier Kabbalah emphasized the role of Israel in bringing about the union and restoration of the upper worlds, here the emphasis shifts from the redeeming of the cosmos to that of the self. The goal of all religious life is *devekut,* the intimate union of the soul with its Source.

This focusing of religion on the inner life needed a system of support. Simply preaching the uplifting of every moment and deed would not suffice. The ancient word *ḥasid* ("pietist;" "lover of God") took on a new meaning in this context, one that it had never previously held in its long history. It now came to mean "disciple." A would-be *ḥasid* was to find a master, a righteous teacher to whom he could entrust his soul. This *tsaddik* or *rebbe* was seen as a holy man, one who would come to know your soul well enough to guide you on your journey and convey to you God's blessing. The community of fellow *ḥasidim* around that *tsaddik* became a sort of mystical fraternity, creating a new model for organization of the Jewish community as a whole.

All of this religious enthusiasm, of course, applied only to the lives of Jews. The belief that God had created the world for His beloved people Israel and longed for their devotion alone is repeated on page after page of the Hasidic homilies. It was clear, usually without having to be stated, that all this discussion of inward perception and moral self-perfection applied only to Jews. Gentiles simply did not have the facility to do it, nor did God require it of them. Yes, halakhic sources considered the non-Jew to be liable to fulfillment of the seven Noahide commandments, but Jews (until Chabad of the 21st century) did not see themselves as responsible in any way for encouraging this.

I find great sadness in the fact that the Jewish and Polish/Ukrainian religious communities, living side by side, were both deeply pious, worshipped the same God, but had nothing positive to do with one another. On the Russian Orthodox side of the divide within Christendom, monasticism was still particularly strong in the 18th century; well-known monasteries existed in some of the same towns that were centers of Hasidism. Truth be told, however, old-style Christian antisemitism was very strong in this area. Both Orthodox priests and Polish Jesuits were frequent perpetrators of the blood libel and other Jew-hating stereotypes, making Jews fear them more than anyone else in their towns and wanting nothing to do with them. It certainly would never have occurred to these Christian clergy that Jews or rabbis had anything of spiritual interest to offer, or that they might be worthy partners in religious conversation. Religion as a zero sum game was fully in effect in Eastern Europe, right down to, and in most cases through, the Holocaust.

In order to give you some sense of the ongoing dichotomy of universal spirituality and tortured exclusivism as they exist within the Hasidic universe, I want to offer fragments of three Hasidic homilies (poetry was not the *métier* of these generations). All three of them come from the same circle, that of the disciples of R. Dov Baer, the *maggid* ("preacher") of Mezritch, who died in 1772. It was from out of his circle that the movement grew. These key authors, R. Elimelech of Lezajsk, R. Menahem Mendel of Vitebsk, and R. Levi Yitshak of Berdychiv were all essential figures in the development of Hasidism. They knew each other well and agreed on most matters.

R. Elimelech took up the role of the Maggid after his death and devoted himself entirely to the training of a new generation of Hasidic leaders, carrying this on until his own passing in 1786. He is considered the father of Hasidism as it spread throughout Poland and Galicia. R. Menahem Mendel emigrated to the Land of Israel in 1777 and founded the Hasidic community there. R. Levi Yitshak served as rabbi of major communities, was known as a great lover and defender of Israel, and became a great figure in later Jewish folklore.

Here is R. Elimelech explaining the efficacy of the *tsaddik*'s prayers, the main reason why ordinary people came to believe in them:

It is known that a *tsaddik's* prayer is answered when praying for a sick person or for others in need. But why? This makes it seem as if the blessed Holy One is subject to change, heaven forbid.[33] But the root of the matter is as follows. The blessed Holy One created letters, which in their original state are pure potential. A *tsaddik* can reconfigure the letters so that they form whatever words are desired. These reconfigurations are what a *tsaddik* does in prayer—making new combinations. The *tsaddik's* prayer does not cause change in the Creator, as the letters were always there. All the *tsaddik* is doing is creating new permutations.

But still you could ask: Why is a *tsaddik's* prayer more effective than the prayer of any other person?… Why couldn't any person pray and reconfigure the letters? This is because the Torah was created with love… **A *tsaddik* loves both God and every person in the world.** For example, "R. Yohanan said: 'I greet every person in the marketplace, including gentiles, before they have a chance to greet me' (b. Berakhot 17a)." Most people are not like this, and therefore they do not have the power to reconfigure the letters. Only a *tsaddik* who loves everyone has that power.[34]

By choosing to quote the Talmudic passage about Rabbi Yo-

---

[33] God's unchanging nature is an axiom of medieval Jewish philosophy. Although not mentioned specifically in Maimonides' Thirteen Articles of Faith, it is taken to be implied by them. This was not consistently the case in earlier biblical or rabbinic Judaism.

[34] No'am Elimelekh, Va-Yishlaḥ. Emphasis mine.

hanan, R. Elimelech makes it clear beyond question that he is indeed speaking of every human being. The *tsaddik's* love is universal, embracing everyone. The letters of the Torah were the source of God's creation of the world; they too embrace all. It is the fact of the *tsaddik's* unbounded love for God and all of Creation, including all people, that enables him to enter into the eternal process of Creation's daily renewal and change the outcome for good.

Next we read a passage by R. Menahem Mendel of Vitebsk, an exquisite description of human love of God, its source, and its transforming power:

> The most essential root of all is [to understand that] you as a person on your own could not perform a single *mitzvah* or good deed, those things that attach you to the ways of Y-H-W-H. It is the Creator who lights up [within you] the fires of love and awe in His presence…
>
> You do not have the power within your mouth even to speak. You do so only by the word of Y-H-W-H, as in "O Lord, open my lips, that my mouth might flow with Your praise (Ps. 51:17)."[35] Both your love and your awe come from God! Then who is the one who loves, if not the living God, flowing through your soul? And whom does He love, if not God? And what is that love? It is hewn out of the flowing essence of divinity. It joins itself and becomes one with the lower world, reducing itself into that microcosm called the human being. Wherever you stand, you are standing within blessed Y-H-W-H, since He is

---

[35] Recited at the opening of each day's three *'amidah* prayers.

the locus of the world, surrounding and filling all the worlds at once.

When that quality of love attacks you, you don't know what is happening. "If you gave all your worldly goods for it, they would shame you (Cant. 8:7)." All is naught in the face of it, because "It comes from Y-H-W-H (Ps. 118:24)." The more you become enraptured, [the more] you will grasp in your heart the truth that this is not your own doing. What have you done? What could you possibly do, given the great coarseness of both your body and mind? This is the spirit of Y-H-W-H speaking within you, His word upon your tongue. This love is a brand plucked from the divine fire. [As you realize this], you will become ever more enflamed, the voice growing louder without ceasing...

In this love you are bound, as a matter of course, to **all who come into this world, to all other humans**, who are just like you. Since such love is a blessing that flows from above, you are absolutely aware that you have not achieved it on your own. You could not have done this at all. Rather the blessed Holy One has given it to you freely. Had God given this gift to another, your fellow-person, they would be just as enflamed [with love] for His great name as you are. That being the case, in what way are you better than your fellow?

...So *of course* you will love **all of Israel**, even the wicked among them, because you truly understand and are aware of how close they are to you. You belong to them. You are just another person; you have nothing over them, other

> than that which has taken you by storm from the heavens.
>
> Therefore, when you rise up in your love of God, they, by the thousands, all rise up with you...You and they constitute a single soul. By whatever rod you can measure, you are tied to those thousands, even tens of thousands, of people. When you rise up, they rise with you.[36]

Notice how seamlessly, in the midst of this truly ecstatic description, the preacher slips from love for all humanity, as the natural and inevitable outcome of God's love, to the love of all Israel. This quite likely was even an unconscious transition. Both *ahavat ha-briot*, love of all people, and *ahavat yisra'el*, the love of all Jews, are key value concepts of the tradition. They are never juxtaposed as contradicting one another, but tend to flow together to become easily interchanged, as is probably the case here. It is impossible to disentangle them here, to understand which of them he intended. That is a reality with which we need to contend within a great many well-meant sources in the Jewish corpus.

Our third text is by R. Levi Yitshak of Berdychiv, the great Lover of Israel. As we will see, in his case that love did not extend beyond the borders of the Jewish community. Here he is in the midst of explaining the Jewish custom of covering one's head, a universally accepted Jewish practice that has no real basis in the Bible or in talmudic law.

> Covering one's head is a gateway to the fear of the Creator and a sense of shame in His presence....
> That is why it is forbidden to us to walk about bare-headed, so that these qualities of shame and awe never depart from us...

---

[36] *Pri ha-Arets*, Shoftim. Emphasis mine.

Israel have this quality of shame that is reflected by our covering our heads. The nations of the world go about bare-headed because they are of insolent spirit. They have no shame; nothing embarrasses them. They have only the audacity represented by their bare heads.

The roots of all personal qualities are in the upper world...The entire people of Israel has this quality of shame; our sages applied it to all of them...[37]

They possess this quality of shame due to the shining down upon them of a light from above, containing all of goodness and the flow of divine desire. This flows upon the entire people of Israel. It is from there that each individual can draw forth these qualities of awe and shame...

But the nations of the world do not engage in acts of Torah or the commandments, for "a gentile who studies Torah deserves to die."[38] He has no portion in it or in its commandments, nor in the roots of those commandments, which are the upper worlds and their holy qualities.[39] Who would bring such a stinking, defiled being into the palace of Y-H-W-H, one uncircumcised of both flesh and heart?

...Lacking the light of these qualities, they are left to be simply creatures of the natural world, born of the four elements and [affected by] their hour of birth. This might lend them a bit of hu-

---

[37] "Israel are shameful, merciful, and doers of good deeds." Yerushalmi Sanhedrin 6:7.
[38] Sanhedrin 59a.
[39] The human moral qualities that derive from the *sefirot*.

man shame. But most are by nature insolent. They remain in that state of nature, like beasts of the forest and audacious dogs.[40]

May the Merciful One make me a person of such shame and awe, all my days.[41]

Here there is no shred of holding back. Levi Yitshak's concept of the *goy* is little different, most likely, from the worst of Ukrainian preachers' or monks' images of the Jews. But there is little comfort to be found in that.

In another sermon found in that same collection, Levi Yitshak offers his own interpretation of a tale we have discussed above, that of God offering His Torah to other nations before giving it to Israel. What sort of special love can God have for Israel, he asks, if He first offered the Torah to the other nations? Edom and Ishmael, representing the Christians and the Muslims, had to turn the Torah down before God offered it to the Jews. Doesn't that make Israel God's third choice, demonstrating that they are of a lower rather than higher status in God's eyes?

Levi Yitshak responds with what is the longest (and indeed somewhat overwritten) parable in this collection of early sermons. There was a king who had great wealth, invested in collections of many sorts of treasures, each kept in a separate treasure house. (One wonders whether he might have seen a treasury like this, as still exist in some once-royal museums in Europe.) One chamber had gold and silver, another contained the royal library, still another a collection of weapons and armaments, and so forth. There was a unique key fitted to open each chamber. The king also had a single and much-beloved legitimate son, to whom he

---

[40] *Kelavim ḥatsufim* is a direct Hebrew rendition of the Aramaic *kalbin de-ḥatsifin* in Luria's poem quoted above.
[41] *Shemu'ah Tovah*, p. 11.

intended to leave all these treasures. To make the son's life easier, the king hired a skilled locksmith to design a master key that would unlock all the treasuries.

It turns out, however, that the king had a number of other children, born of concubines rather than of the queen. He feared that these would one day become deadly rivals to his son. To prevent that, he called one of them aside and offered him that master key. He did not tell him, however, that it would open any of the chambers he chose. "Because you are so dear to me," the king said to this son, "I want you to have this key to my collections."

The fact was, however, that this son had been stealing from the king for a long time. He was so racked with guilt that when he saw the key, he immediately thought he was being asked to open the roomful of armaments and would be forced to choose the weapon with which he would be punished. Without trying the key in any lock, he gave it back, saying that he was not worthy of this parental gift. Each of the other illegitimate sons did the same (in other words, they were *all* stealing from the king), until finally the king could give it to his only true son without fear of competition or complaint.

The meaning of the parable is obvious. God had no real interest in giving Torah to anyone but Israel. When each of the other nations asked what was in it, God intentionally mentioned that thing He knew would make them reject it, as recounted in the midrashic source. The nations, in other words, have a relationship with God that is solely based on guilt and fear. But when God then offered the Torah to Israel, He showed them the nature of the special key. In contrast to his attempt to somewhat deceive the others, he spoke to this true son with his heart fully open, without any attempt at deceit. The passion of true love was then awakened between them.

The midrashic story that originally served as an apologetic for the election of Israel—God did indeed offer His Torah to the nations, but only we accepted it—has now been turned around to serve the very opposite purpose, showing that God never had the slightest intent of truly offering it to anyone but His only true son. He just had to remove the objections of these illegitimate offspring. Had God spoken to the Gentiles at Sinai, Levi Yitsḥak suggests elsewhere, they would have stood as still and unmoved as trees or rocks since they have "not a drop of holiness within them," while Israel were so agitated that they felt their souls would depart from them.[42] Jews have within them an imprint of holiness that cannot be erased, but "the Gentiles have no relationship to anything that is holy, only to superficial things." This makes them fickle in their loyalties, as he says, "Even when one of them acts well and directs himself to become attached to something holy, as soon as he backslides, he will be cut off from it entirely. The holy will make no impression on him. The gentiles have no essential or true relationship to holiness, only one that can come about by chance."[43]

Let it be clear that this is the same R. Levi Yitsḥak whom I love for so many other reasons that I have spent years studying his teachings. I recently wrote a whole book about him,[44] which some scholars will undoubtedly criticize as being too sympathetic. I am saddened to discover some of the awful things R. Levi Yitsḥak said about gentiles, but I cannot allow this to diminish my love for this great lover of Jews. That realization does force me, however, to look again at Christians' veneration of figures including Martin Luther, Pius XII, and so many others whose love did not extend beyond their own community of faith. An uncomfortable feeling.

This text, incidentally, appeared in print only in the 20th century. It was published in Warsaw in 1938, just a year before the

---

[42] *Kedushat Levi* 2:103–4, *va-etḥanan*.
[43] *Shemu'ah Tovah* 40a.
[44] *Defender of the Faithful* (Brandeis University Press, 2023).

war and the German occupation. Supposedly, only five copies survived the Holocaust, one of them serving as the basis for a photo-offset edition in post-war New York. The manuscript from which it was printed was lost with all the rest of the Kozienicer rebbe's large library, in the ashes of the Holocaust.

In Levi Yitshak's own day, every Hebrew book that was published in the czarist empire contained the following statement, usually published right on the title page, sometimes on its reverse side:

IMPORTANT ANNOUNCEMENT: Let it be known that everyplace in this book where the term idolator, gentile, alien, or "nations of the world" might appear, the reference is to nations that existed in antiquity. It is to them that the words of our Torah and the interpretations of our sages applied. But the people in whose shadow we live today worship the Maker of heaven and earth. They are pious, believing in Creation and the essentials of religion. God forbid that we should think or even consider any ill will toward them! Did King David himself not pray only that You "pour out Your wrath on those nations that do not know You and the kingdoms that do not call upon Your name"[45]... Not only do we not bear any ill will toward them, but we are obliged to pray for their welfare and success...[46]

Of course, such a statement was intended for the eyes of the censor, not because anyone thought to take it seriously.[47]

Hasidism is the last major creative movement in Jewish history prior to the full impact of modernity. Although historians now describe it as an early modern movement, its origins lie in the full and unquestioning inheritance of the whole prior tradition, read in an atmosphere of intensive personal and mystical piety. This brought along with it all the best and the worst that the long tradition had to offer.

This is the place to summarize our brief journey through the

---

[45] Ps. 79:6, quoted in the Passover Haggadah, where no one thinks that it refers to the nations of antiquity.

[46] Translation abbreviated from that found on the verso of the title page in R. Hayyim Tirer's *Sidduro shel Shabbat*, Mohilev, 1817, pictured here.

[47] As this book goes to press, the Daf Yomi has just completed the tractate 'Avodah Zarah. My email feed received, just today, the following notice:

Translators of this tractate suggest that the rules around contact with idol worshippers and the idols themselves have been nullified, reasoning that "Negative remarks in this tractate about the morals of idol worshippers were descriptive of the pagans whose depraved behavior the Sages observed, and should not be construed as pertaining to any of the cultured societies in which we reside nowadays."

You decide whether you believe them.

intellectual/religious history of Jewry in pre-modern times. We have seen that both the universalist and national elements within the biblical heritage, represented by the two psalms, continued to exist over the centuries when Jews experienced persecution and oppression. We have noted that Jewish isolation from the surrounding societies was the result of both exclusion from without and self-protective choice from within. With the passing of centuries, the universalist stream came to focus more on God as universal Creator and less on a universalist view of humanity. The national side, ever more wounded by the painful course of history, became embittered, depicting the nations of the world either as illegitimate heirs or as vicious beasts, ready to set upon Israel, innocent lamb, eternal victim.

The Divergence of East and West and the Zionism of Each

Why is it, you may ask, that I have heard so little about this sort of Judaism? The simple answer is that most of us Western Jews have been informed by a highly selective reading of the tradition that first emerged in the early 19th century. It was given an interesting new name, that of *Mainstream Judaism*. This was a term and concept that had never existed previously. (Still, by the way, it is a term that cannot quite be translated into Hebrew, in which it is called *yahadut maynstrim*.) Judaism had always been a cumulative tradition, reinterpreting constantly, but never admitting that it selected one part of its legacy while rejecting others.

Around the second decade of the 19th century, as the Enlightenment brought forth the first generation of critical and historical Judaic scholars, they wanted to present to the Western world a face of Judaism that it might find attractive, or at least tolerable. They did so by means of somewhat arbitrary choices of what was considered part of the Jewish "mainstream," and what was considered secondary to it, therefore liable to being swept under the rug. In short, beliefs, ideas and practices that they thought would be embarrassing to Jews entering into Western society were ignored and set aside. These included the entire mystical tradition, alongside folk beliefs that were considered to be superstitions. The Hasidic veneration of *tsaddikim* and belief in their miraculous powers certainly had no place in a Judaism for the modern world. Sometimes these beliefs were derided as simple nonsense, better to be forgotten. In other situations, they were attributed to non-Jewish sources, things Judaism had "picked up along the way" in the course of its long exile, but that were not an essential part of the tradition. The ideal faithful Jew in these circles was none other than Moses Mendelssohn, a champion of Western enlightenment, who thought in wholly Western philosophical categories, but nevertheless remained loyal to the traditional Jewish way of life. The old phrase regarding Moses Maimonides, "From Moses to Moses there arose no one like Moses," was now extended to this third Moses, the ideal figure of the pious but westernized Jew.[48]

This modern and highly selective reading of Jewish tradition took place first in Germany. As Jews moved westward from the old Eastern European homeland into German- and English-speaking environments, this *Wissenschaft* understanding of Judaism was highly successful in displacing what were seen as more "primitive" or old-fashioned forms of religion. Jews were moving from a part of the world where they had seen themselves as among the more educated and literate sections of society, with the surrounding culture mostly an illiterate peasant one, into areas where these immigrants and their children aspired to nothing more than to reach the high cultural level of the society into which they had come. Russian and Polish Jews moving westward soaked in the culture of middle Europe, and then of England and America, seeking to make it their own. Second and third generation Jews in western lands were anxious not only to imitate, but to creatively participate in the cultural life of those societies. And so we did. But doing so, becoming fully acculturated to the West meant leaving many things behind, including Jewish languages and large parts of the tradition, alongside mannerisms and styles of self-expression.

As this westernized definition of Judaism moved from the

---

[48] Abraham Joshua Heschel confided in me, sometime in the 1960s, that the Jewish Theological Seminary's chancellor had told him that he could not teach Hasidism as part of his required teaching load, because "Hasidism is not part of mainstream Judaism."

small circle of scholars into the wider community, it came to exist in both Reform and Orthodox versions. On the Reform side, it meant that Judaism was to be seen clearly as a universalist and progressive expression of ethical monotheism. Its advantage over Christianity, which was an important trope, was the fact that its pure monotheistic faith was compromised neither by trinitarianism nor by physical representation of the deity. Its values, however, were very much in line with those of a liberal, enlightened Protestantism. Both in Germany (Hermann Cohen) and in the United States, Reform Judaism sought to emphasize the ethical teachings of the prophets, indeed, to depict contemporary Judaism as a direct descendant of that prophetic message, more so than of the talmudic rabbis. Religious practices that were post-biblical in origin were considered dispensable. Anything that smacked of either mysticism or Hasidism was total anathema.

For the Orthodox, the situation was quite different. *Halakhah*, represented by the authority of the *Shulḥan 'Arukh* and its ongoing interpreters, remained in force and unquestioned. That did not mean, however, that all the beliefs and uncodified customs that accompanied it were to be accepted without question. Modern Orthodoxy mostly accepted the model offered by Mendelssohn, who insisted that Judaism differed from other forms of enlightened religion by its code of praxis, but not by its beliefs. Even a rigorously pious figure like Rabbi Samson Raphael Hirsch, active in the late 19th century, stood very far culturally from the East European Judaism of his day, despite being fully observant of *halakhah* and even agreeing to separate his Orthodox community entirely from those he saw as assimilationists.

A significant part of world Jewry, however, did not participate in that process. These were the Jews who stayed at home in Eastern Europe, both those who remained Orthodox[49] and those who

---

[49] The word "Orthodox" for traditionally observant Jews was an invention

abandoned that tradition in favor of Zionism or other ideologies. Even those who left the tradition behind (and so too their Israeli grandchildren today) still understood "real" Judaism to be that of the talmudic and medieval legacy, as passed on through the channels of both Kabbalah and Hasidism. They simply had no interaction with the face of Judaism that we in the West considered "mainstream."

Jews in traditional East European Jewish communities, especially before urbanization, bore a sense of superiority to the surrounding Polish, Ukrainian, or Belorussian peasantry. Part of this may be seen as a defensive inversion of the pervasive Jew-hatred of the society, so strongly fostered by the Church. Another part may be attributed to the illiteracy and backwardness that characterized the peasantry, which was looked down upon by educated non-Jews as well. But some of it also derives from long-existing theological conceptions, festering within Jewish populations where circumstance seemed to confirm them.

So too the Jewish communities of North Africa and the Near East. The Judaism they inherited was essentially that of the pre-modern world, mostly untouched by this veneer of westernization. When groups like the Alliance Israelite or ORT came in to educate the youth of these communities, they sought to give them the skills, both linguistic and technical, to function in the modern world. But the understanding of Judaism itself was beyond their reach. They preferred to avoid conflict over that, leaving it in the hands of the rabbis, who themselves were educated only in the most traditional fashion. All those aspects of Judaism, including both Kabbalah and popular religion, that

---

of the mid-19th century. It came to be widely used in Germany and in the vast Jewish populations of the Hapsburg empire. It never quite worked for Jews in Russia, since the word was already linked with a different meaning, that of Orthodox Christianity. There the faithful just described themselves as that which they had always been, *shomrey Torah u-mitsvos*.

had been set aside in the West were and are still alive and well among them.

The major Ashkenazic part of that Jewish population, of course, was obliterated in the Holocaust. Over five million of the six million Jews were Polish or Russian/Ukrainian.[50] The survivors bore the scars that helped confirm for them all the worst that the tradition had to say about the world of the Gentiles. Those who remained religious tended toward extremism, often far beyond that of their pre-war parents and grandparents. The shock they had experienced caused them to draw away from the outside world as much as possible, and into the cocoon of closed religious communities, surrounded by the highest sort of walls they could erect. This was true of the survivors who chose to settle both in Israel and in America. This became the core of the *ḥaredi* community as it exists today, in both its Hasidic and "Lithuanian" versions.

For those who had given up on religion, either before the Holocaust or because of it, the image of Judaism they had was of something negative and backward, a burden they were eager to leave behind. The new values to which they aspired, whether Zionist, socialist, or some combination of the two, included great emphasis on personal liberty, especially freedom *from* religion. A non-religious Jew was called in Yiddish a *freyer*, a "free" or "liberated" person. (The word later took on an entirely different meaning in Israeli Hebrew.)

The definition of the tradition from which they had liberated themselves, however, remained in the hands of the ultra-Orthodox. A sort of conspiracy existed between them and the Jewish secularists. The latter were happy to see Judaism presented in

---

[50] Another million and a half were the majority of Soviet Jews, who were forced to abandon and then quite quickly forgot almost any knowledge of Jewish tradition, except for some folk beliefs and attitudes, including a whiff of intellectual superiority, that did survive among them.

its most unabashed and "primitive" way. This justified their own decision to leave it behind. How could one believe in such nonsense? It has been suggested that liberal Judaism is a product of Protestant societies and the experience of living as a minority within them. In the Protestant universe, if you don't like a particular church, you create a new one, perhaps even building it next door. In the universe of Catholicism and Eastern Orthodoxy, there exists no such possibility. The Church is the Church; if you are opposed to it, you declare yourself an atheist. Thus, non-Orthodox forms of Judaism did not develop in Russia, Poland, or France. Germany and the United States, the homelands of liberal Judaism, are essentially Protestant societies.

The Sephardic and *Mizraḥi* communities that immigrated to Israel in the early years of the state were in varying stages in the process of modernization. The Jews of Baghdad were much further along than their neighbors in the Kurdish communities to their north. Among the Moroccans, there was a great difference between those from the urbanized north and those coming from the towns of the Atlas mountains. But the religion they all knew as Judaism was one deeply imbued with Kabbalah, often in its most popular and quasi-magical form. Pilgrimages to graves of saints, amulets, and the blessings of holy men continue to play a role in the lives of those who remain faithful to that part of the tradition. Even among those for whom full religious observance has declined in these communities, such folk beliefs remain strong.

The Holy Land itself had always played a major role in the dreams and aspirations of those communities. Unlike the earlier immigrants from Europe, who created a mostly secular culture in the Land of Israel, these Jews saw their "ascent" to the land in sacred and semi-messianic ways. Their dream was a holy land centered in a rebuilt Jerusalem, in contrast to the *ḥalutzim*, the pioneers, who shunned the Holy City, caring much more for the rich farming plains of the Jezreel Valley.

Elements of all of these communities brought along with them a sense of Jewish spiritual and intellectual superiority. In their encounter with the Arab population of Palestine, we read rather little about the sophisticated and highly literate upper-class Arabs in such cities as Jerusalem, Cairo, or Beirut. Palestinians, in the eyes of Jewish immigrants to the land, from the beginning, were the *falahin*, ignorant peasants, not unlike those they had left (or fled) back home.[51] Occasionally they were romanticized in the writing of Jewish authors in the early years, but usually they were either the enemy (which many of them had indeed chosen to be) or just "background noise" to the great undertaking of the Return to Zion and the Redemption of the Land.

The division within Jewry that I am suggesting here is not a usual one. It is not between Ashkenazi and Sefaradi/*Mizraḥi*, nor is it between Israelis and Diaspora Jews. It is between those whose understanding of Judaism itself has been modified by the lens of westernization, and those who see the tradition essentially in its premodern form. The latter include, I am suggesting, both those Eastern European Jews whose view of Judaism did not go through, or rejected, a certain modernization process, as well as most of the Jewish communities of the Near East. It may include many people who are no longer observant, even those who call themselves atheists, but still understand the tradition itself as it existed up to the 19th century, when so many chose to leave it behind. Because of the two great events of Jewish history in the first half of the 20th century—emigration to the West, especially North America, and the Holocaust—Jews are almost equally divided between these two groups. The modernists in their understanding of Judaism are dominant in America, except for the several hundred thousand Hasidic and other ultra-Orthodox

---

[51] Exceptions to this existed in some of the old-time Sephardic families in the land, but they had little impact on the great waves of immigrants to come.

(mostly descendants of Holocaust survivors) in New York and a few other centers, along with a growing circle around them. In Israel, the traditionalist understanding of what constitutes Judaism holds the center, except among English-speaking immigrants, members of the few liberal synagogues, and some descendants of middle-European Jews.

Zionism emerged in the late 19th century out of two circles, one Western/Central European and the other within the Russian empire (which then still included Poland). Theodore Herzl, Max Nordau, and Chaim Weizmann were all very much Western Jews. Whatever knowledge of Judaism they had came through the westernizing filter of the "mainstream." For them, their Zionist self-discovery was a response to the inability of Jews to truly be accepted into the middle and upper classes of emerging Western society. Even though Jews in Germany and westward seemed to have given up a great deal of what made them different from others, antisemitism was thriving. Indeed, it was of a new sort. No longer primarily religious in an open sense, it drew on resentment of Jewish achievement and economic competition. Jews succeeded greatly in both business and professions once they were given an even partially equal playing field. But in their success, they seemed able to create parallel social and cultural institutions to those around them much more easily than they could be accepted into the existing ones. Enlightenment, which had originally been thought of as an ongoing process, seemed stalled by growing nationalism and romanticism. These tended to exclude the Jews. The Dreyfus Affair in France, the election of Karl Lueger as openly antisemitic mayor of Vienna, and other such events shook them deeply. In America, the exclusion of Jews from hotels, resorts, country clubs, etc. felt like a clear statement that we were "not wanted." Antisemitism clearly persevered, even in the *goldene medine*, the great new homeland Jews had found across the sea. The idea of creating a Jewish society in our own ancient homeland, especially such a polite and liberal one as Herzl described in his novel *Altneuland*, began to attract a following.

Russian Zionism was an entirely different story. The situation of Jews in the Russian empire felt desperate. The pogroms that had begun in 1881 had created a tremendous sense of insecurity, especially in the shtetls and the countryside. Large numbers of Jews moved from small towns to major cities, in search of both livelihood and the security of living in larger Jewish communities. Equally large numbers were choosing the path of emigration, primarily to the United States, but also to England and western Europe. There was a feeling that this was a moment of choice for the Jewish people. Urbanization in Russia and Poland often meant both secularization and cultural assimilation. This was a moment when many left religion behind. The question was where one would turn for a new orientation and set of values, once that took place.

A powerful alternative to Zionism in Eastern Europe was the Jewish workers' movement, represented most by the Bund. In the cities, where Jews worked under sweatshop conditions, the labor movement and emerging socialism were attracting large numbers of Jewish followers. It stood for a Yiddish-speaking Jewish national identity tied to the values of socialism. Bundists and other such groups fought for Jewish workers' rights against both government officials and factory owners (mostly Jews themselves), but also cultivated the growth of a secular world of Yiddish culture. They believed that Jews should stay where they were and work for the betterment of all, rather than separating themselves from other workers around them by going off to the Land of Israel. The ultimate defeat of Bundism came only with the obliteration of most of its followers in the Holocaust.

By the early 20th century, large numbers of Jews in the cities were also beginning to raise their children to speak Russian or

Polish, rather than Yiddish. As the alternative of secular lifestyle became accessible, there was a fear that distinctive Jewish identity, for the multitudes abandoning religious observance, would disappear. Concern arose also that assimilation would be even more the case in the new lands where Jews were settling. Would the millions of souls emigrating to America be lost to the Jewish people? Zionism emerged in Russia in large part as an alternative to assimilation. It sought both a political solution to Jewish powerlessness and a new sort of Jewish identity, anchored in the revived Hebrew language and a sense of national renewal that came with it.

The key figures of Russian Zionism, Ahad ha-'Am (Asher Ginzberg) on one hand and Rabbi Isaac Reines on the other, both thought of Zionism as an opportunity for the cultural and spiritual rebirth of the Jewish people. A new Jewish center in the land of Israel would bring about, along with the revival of the Hebrew language, an era of literary, artistic, and spiritual renewal. Poets like Bialik and Tshernichowsky and the cultural creativity that they, and many other new Hebrew writers, inspired were key to this dream. That center would serve to reinvigorate Jewish life in the Diaspora as well, giving it an aura of hope in the possibility of a creative future, rather than just living from one pogrom or insult to the next.

In the decades-long campaign to sell Zionism in both east and west, its spokesmen did not hesitate to dip into the rich symbolic language of tradition. Zionism was depicted as *ge'ulah*, redemption, saving Jews from the ongoing depredations of life in *galut*. *Galut*, or exile, is understood in the tradition as resulting from the destruction of the ancient Temple and the exiling (although much of it was probably voluntary migration) of the Jews from their homeland. It represented *a period of history*, that between the destruction and the advent of Messiah. But in the new Hebrew vocabulary that was springing up inside the Zionist movement, the word *galut* now took the form *golah*, and its opposite was *ge'ulah*, redemption, which meant *'aliyah* or immigration to the Land of Israel. A Jew who made the decision to move from Kyiv or Odessa to Tel Aviv or the Jezreel Valley was considered "redeemed." For them, the *galut* was over. This is a tremendous shift in the meaning of a key symbol of Judaism. It is not historic *time* that is divided between eras of destruction and redemption. Instead, it is *space* that is divided, between the exilic state of living outside the Land and the "redeemed" state of returning to it. The same use of redemption was applied to the Land itself. The Jewish National Fund, established already in the first decade of the 20th century, to which Jews from throughout the Diaspora contributed, was dedicated primarily to acquisition of land for Jewish settlers, mostly through purchase from Turkish or Arab landlords. The slogan of JNF has always been "Bring Redemption to the Land," a biblical verse from the book of Leviticus (25:24), which is actually talking about holding on to one's land during observance of the sabbatical year. But in Zionist parlance, Jewish ownership meant "redemption."

Major opposition to Zionism came primarily from the rabbinate, both Orthodox and Reform. For the Orthodox, especially in Eastern Europe, and even more so from the Hasidic rebbes, the taking of Jewish fate into our own hands was seen as a violation of the messianic dream. Yes, the Jews would go back to the Land of Israel, but only when Messiah led us there. The idea of giving up on waiting for his coming, as Jews had been doing for 2,000 years, was considered a violation of trust in God. The fact that the Zionist effort was being led by people who were openly rebellious against traditional religious observance sealed the deal as far as the rabbis were concerned. The second *'aliyah* (wave of immigration), beginning in the opening decade of the 20th century, was primarily secular and socialist in orientation. The rabbinate identified with the old ultra-Orthodox community of Jerusalem, that saw these people as anathema. Rabbi Reines and his new Mizrachi party of religious Zionists represented a small minority within the rabbinic leadership of Eastern Europe. The objection on the Reform side was entirely different. Liberal Judaism in Europe, and even more so in America, had insisted on giving up on the sense of Jewish peoplehood as a collective and potentially political identity. Jews were German or American "citizens of the Jewish faith." Judaism was to model itself as a religion, based on the prevalent Protestant Christian understanding of that term. Any notion that Judaism was about national identity might threaten the loyalty of Jews to their respective countries. That would only reinforce the antisemitic stereotypes being put forth quite actively by those who read and reprinted the *Protocols of the Elders of Zion*. Jews as such had no political loyalties or interests. That notion could not be threatened.

All this changed dramatically after Hitler's rise to power in 1933 and even more so when the fate of German Jewry became clear in 1938. Jews were desperate to get out of Europe. The willingness of the growing community in Palestine to welcome and accept more of them came to be seen as the great task to be supported by Jews around the world. How could one not support such an effort? Other countries, including Britain and the United States, were clearly not willing to accept large numbers of Jewish immigrants, even if it was a matter of saving lives. There was Palestine, the ideal place for a Jew to go. It was only the Arabs and the British who seemed to stubbornly stand in the way of this life-saving response to a growing life-or-death emergency.

At that point, opposition to Zionism disappeared throughout most of the world Jewish community. In Europe, only the most ultra-Orthodox corners within eastern Europe, mostly Hasidic, continued to resist. They were widely criticized—even hated by some—after the war, for having encouraged their faithful to remain, especially in Hungary, when there was still time to flee.

In America, Reform Judaism made a major change in supporting Zionism, expressed by such important figures as Stephen Wise and Abba Hillel Silver. Only a small group of the most assimilationist corner within American Reform, organized around the American Council for Judaism, continued to question Zionism.

After the war, with the full horror of the Holocaust just being revealed bit by bit and tens of thousands of Jews gathering in Displaced Persons camps, it was completely clear that large scale immigration to Palestine was the only solution for these desperately battered and needy people. Western countries were willing to accept only a few of them at a rather slow pace, but the need was immediate. Therefore, virtually the entire world Jewish community strongly supported the notion of *'aliyah* and bitterly opposed the British Mandate restrictions on it. By the time of the United Nations Partition Plan in 1947, and the threats of Arab nations to invade if a Jewish state was proclaimed, world Jewry was on board to support the embattled *yishuv*, including vast financial help and even providing arms in various (technically illegal) ways.

For Jews throughout the world, the victory in 1948 was presented as something of a miracle. Whether one used that term in its literal sense, betokening divine intervention, or not, it was hard to imagine a rough-hewn group of Jewish pioneers, including many just off the boat from the concentration camps, setting back the armies of seven Arab countries. We were told nothing of the forced displacement of Palestinians by the Palmach or other emerging Israeli armed forces. As far as we knew, many Palestinians had chosen to flee, often at the behest of Arab spokesmen and radio announcers. They had been promised they could return soon and slaughter the Jews, as soon as the Arab armies were victorious. The notion of 1948 as a *naqba* or tragedy for the Palestinian people was completely unknown or unnoticed. It is now clear that this hiding was intentional, a decision of the Ben

Gurion government.

For the next 19 years, until 1967, support for Israel and pride in its truly tremendous achievements were central to the self-definition of Jews around the world. There was a growing sense that having a Jewish state, which would stand up for Jews persecuted anywhere, was essential to our own existence. The implication was that had such a state existed prior to the rise of Hitler the Holocaust might have been prevented. While that is by no means necessarily the case, it certainly felt that way to a still shell-shocked Jewish people.

Among those great achievements was the absorption of immigrants, both from the DP camps of Europe and from Muslim-dominated countries around the Mediterranean and throughout the Near East. As we learned of their difficulties and sufferings in temporary immigrant housing, we were encouraged to contribute even greater sums of money to Israel, for their settlement and integration. An increasingly successful and high-earning Jewish community in the capitalist United States was taught to love the socialist experiment of the kibbutzim, respecting their great role in the creation of a new Israeli economy, including agriculture, a venture so new to most Jews. Diaspora Jewish communities organized around synagogues, especially the non-Orthodox ones, came to accept the fact that the Israel they supported was a mostly secular society, a place that seemed to have no need for religion as the means of Jewish identity. There was some discomfort around this, but we were reassured by the fact that this secular majority seemed to maintain the same sort of universal moral values that we liberal Jews (and Jewish liberals) all attributed to our tradition.

We understood that there was a religious minority within the Israeli population, numbering about 20–25%. In retrospect, it is now clear that these numbers were totally distorted, based on the old Eastern European model of counting people as either fully

Orthodox or "secular." The vast *mizraḥi* Jewish population, soon to become a majority within Israel, remained traditionalist in its attitudes, as we have seen, even without a fully Orthodox regimen of praxis. Among those counted as religious, there was a divide between the Zionist Orthodox and the non-Zionist *ḥaredim*. The former seemed to be led by people who shared in Western values, such as Moshe Shapira and Joseph Burg. Their interests were mostly sectoral, preserving public observance of the Sabbath and *kashrut*, and especially keeping issues of personal and marital status within the domain of the chief rabbinate, which was also dominated by such relatively progressive figures as rabbis Herzog and Ouziel. The *ḥaredim* were off in a corner of their own, rebuilding both families and *yeshivot* destroyed during the war, and were seen as a benign curiosity, certainly not a threat to anyone.

1967, Victory and Defeat

The Six Day War changed everything. I remember a Hebrew teacher of mine saying, back in the 1950s, that he considered it an act of God (he meant it in a mostly metaphorical sense) that we had not succeeded in capturing the Old City of Jerusalem in 1948. Possession of the Temple Mount, he said, would have divided the Jewish people so bitterly that it was a blessing to see it remain in Arab hands. Note that he was not speaking of Jewish-Arab conflict over the mount, but about the division it would cause *among Jews*.

I was ordained as a rabbi on Sunday, June 4, 1967, the day before the Six Day War broke out. The graduation speaker at the Jewish Theological Seminary was Elie Wiesel. It was a moment of high drama. We were all terrified that Israel was about to be overrun by Egyptian and Syrian forces. Over the course of the preceding decade, Holocaust awareness had grown tremendously within the Jewish community and in the Western world at large. This felt like we were on the eve of another possible Holocaust. When the war broke out, friends of mine got onto planes to Israel as soon as they could, to help in the management of civil society, including picking crops and collecting trash, while Israelis went to war. I was a budding rare book collector at the time, and I sold a number of my treasures to be able to contribute to the effort. Everyone, from poor students like me to those with greatest resources, gave what they could.

The quick victory again felt like a miracle. This time, however, it took on a much more religious character then it had in 1948. The symbol of the '48 war had been the *Davidka*, the simple cannon that helped so much in the battle for the Israeli New City of Jerusalem. The symbol of this war was nothing less than the Western Wall itself, revered by Jews as the last remnant of the Second Temple. Ironically, although the war had been fought and won largely by the children of Palmach veterans, including many from the secular kibbutzim, the victory was celebrated most in both the Zionist religious and *mizrahi* communities. They were the ones for whom victory meant not only the saving of Israel from destruction, but possession of the Holy City and its shrine. Their emblem of that victory became not the picture of the young soldiers who conquered the city, but that of Rabbi Goren carrying a Torah scroll to the site.

Among the loudest celebrators of the victory were disciples of Rabbi Zvi Yehudah Kook, son of the great mystic and teacher Rabbi Abraham Isaac Kook (d. 1935) and leader of the yeshiva in Jerusalem that bore his name. This Jerusalem yeshiva was the main training ground of rabbis for the religious Zionist community. Over the two preceding decades, the thought of the elder Rabbi Kook had become the dominant ideology of that segment of the Israeli population. Kook had been known as an Orthodox East European rabbi of the old school who embraced the secular *yishuv* and saw it as a positive step in the ongoing redemption of the Jewish people. For him as well, the use of that word "redemption" bore within it a definite messianic implication. Kook had at least a strong faith in the imminent arrival of Messiah. Some understand him as having made a claim for himself as having a key role in the messianic drama.

Rav Kook died before the Holocaust. His son, looking back over Jewish and world history from 1935 to 1967, became utterly convinced that this drama was unfolding before our eyes. The more intellectual part of the Orthodox community, including its rabbinate, had been struggling terribly to understand the meaning of all that had happened in that period of time, including the seeming absence of God during the most terrible years of Jewish history. Rav Zvi Yehudah and others around him began to put a picture together that gave it all meaning. The Holocaust had been nothing other than the long-announced terrible "birth pangs of Messiah" announcing a new and transformative era. The miracles of 1948 and 1967 had to be treated precisely as that, interventions by the divine hand into the historical process. The redemption of Israel was now at hand and we had to do everything to become full participants in it.

Here a word needs to be added regarding the varying notions of the messianic age among Jews in the eastern and western divisions of the Jewish world described above. Westernized Jews had long accepted a full universalization of the messianic vision laid out by the ancient prophets of Israel. Indeed, there was biblical basis for this. Isaiah and others had spoken of an age when all the nations would lay down their weapons and an era of universal peace would ensue. Christianity, reading some of those same verses in Isaiah, had certainly presented the redemption that way. Christ was depicted as the "Prince of Peace," based on a figure described in the prophetic tradition. While liberal Jews did not accept the identification of this figure with Jesus, they came to share a notion of a future redeemed world with the rest of western society. The redemption of Israel (here meaning the Jewish people) from its suffering was both a first step and a symbolic example of that coming universal new age.

For a large segment of world Jewry, the socialist and even communist visions of a transformed society had great appeal as secular transformations of this messianic hope. Emerging in the decades prior to Zionism, they had in common with it an understanding that we could no longer wait for God to bring about this redemption; we had to take the task into human hands, with all their mortal fallibility. Needless to say, that attempt brought catastrophe to a large part of the world. The dreams of that secular redemption and loyalty to it died among Jews both in Israel and the United States, where it once had wide support. In Israel this was marked by the decline of the kibbutzim and the socialist vision that had idealized them, seeing them as the vanguard of the future. In America, as well as in Israel, the increased opening of opportunity to do very well in the capitalist society did much to snuff out the last embers of the socialist dream. In the US, the McCarthyism of the postwar era was a final nail in its coffin.

But for the larger traditionalist Eastern European and Mediterranean parts of the Jewish community, messianism had always meant something very different. It was all about the redemption of Israel, who apparently were to have a dominant or at least highly significant role in the era to come. The Messiah, after all, was to be a Jew, descended from the House of David. The Holy Land was to be seen as the center of the world, with peoples everywhere turning toward Jerusalem. Jewish rule over the entire Land of Israel was seen to be essential to that redemption. More and more, the foretold redemption of Israel, the People, came to be identified with Israel, the State.

Originally, of course, that rule was to have been brought about by Messiah himself, who would conquer the Holy Land from the heathens. But now, it appeared, God had chosen to unfold the drama in somewhat unexpected ways. For reasons unfathomable to us, He placed the return to Zion in the hands of impious Jewish leaders. They created the great Israeli army that had brought about the victory, enabling us to become rulers of the land. Messiah was to come, for sure, but the order of events was different than that which had been predicted. Rav Kook's teachings offered a path toward understanding things that way. His influence extended to parts of the secular Israeli population as well.

Meanwhile, achieving full Jewish sovereignty over the land was something we could do in preparation. The Palestinian

Arabs, many of whom had lived there for countless generations (though there was always a good deal of migration to and fro within the Middle East) were simply in the way. They did not have a place in this vision of the land that belonged to the Jews alone. In some very extreme quarters, they were drawn as parallel to the seven ancient nations of Canaan, whom Moses had been commanded to exterminate. This was not the norm, however, even in national religious circles. The rabbis of the Talmud had already declared that those nations no longer existed. Still, the very violent descriptions of our original conquest, recorded especially in the Book of Joshua, were part of our sacred canon, rediscovered (after long neglect) by Zionist educators. In any case, the Arab population was an obstacle in the way of total Jewish mastery over the land. Ways would have to be found to deal with it, including the hope that sufficiently miserable living conditions would encourage them to emigrate across the Jordan or elsewhere, "voluntarily." The idea of forced transfer remained "beyond the pale" for most Israelis, even those on the right, except for the most extreme. At least until now, when that extreme right has come to run the country.

Leaving the Messiah aside for the moment, this emphasis on a Jewish-only population for the Land of Israel has a familiarity that echoes strongly for those familiar with recent Jewish history. Considering this analogy might be helpful. When Poland, absent from the political map of Europe for over a century, was reconstituted by the Versailles treaty of 1918, the Poles found to their distress that they had a population that was 25% non-Polish. This included about 3 million Jews, 10% of the population, and over 4 million Ukrainians in the eastern provinces and Germans in the west. The Poles were not happy about these minorities in their new country. As fascism grew rampant in Poland in the mid-1930s, the fascist parties turned rabidly antisemitic. Their main goal was to get Jews to emigrate in any way possible. This even included a degree of collaboration with right-wing Zionist factions, hoping to increase immigration to Palestine. The Poles, too, were not willing either to exterminate the Jews or to just dump them out of the country off the backs of trucks. But there were clearly people among them who would have relished the thought. How quickly we forget!

Israel's highly controversial "nation-state bill," passed in 2018 by the Likud (Netanyahu's party) majority, states that in the Land of Israel (meaning all of it) national rights of self-expression belong exclusively to the Jewish people. To exemplify this, it demoted the status of Arabic, until then legally a co-equal language with Hebrew in the state, to secondary status.

The Yom Kippur war of 1973 came as a shock to all Israelis. Suddenly, memory of the quick victory of seven years earlier seemed distant. But it was particularly distressing to the growing messianic cadre, who saw it as a setback in the divine plan for history that was emerging before their eyes. In response to it, disciples of R. Zvi Yehudah Kook created a movement called *Gush Emunim*, the bloc of the faithful. They became actively involved in an effort toward the full settlement of Jews in both the West Bank and Gaza, which had already begun by 1969. Their aim was to make it clear that Israel could never even consider pulling out of these territories, which they considered part of the Land of Israel, as it had from the vast reaches of Sinai in the peace treaty with Egypt that happened during that time. They presented themselves as a new generation of pioneers, willing to take up the hardship and danger of living in the territories, supposedly sacrificing the more comfortable and safer environment of homes within the Green Line, the state's border until 1967. This element of pioneering and the building of new settlements had been so much a part of the Zionist vision since the early 20th century that even so-called left-wing governments could not bring themselves to shut it down.

Many people, both within Israel and throughout the Diaspora, were upset by this development and saw it as a tremendous error, both moral and strategic, for the Jewish state. We (I include myself within that group since about 1969) understood that the territories belonged to the Palestinians and should be preserved for them under Israeli administration until a Palestinian political leadership emerged that was willing to make true peace with Israel. Then these lands would form the basis of a Palestinian state. But we were told, quite forcefully, by representatives of various Israeli governments, to shut up. How dare we diaspora Jews express ideas on a subject that related, after all, to Israel's security. Were our sons and daughters fighting on the front lines? But, over the years, a great deal of oppression and land-grabbing have been hidden behind that blanket of "security."

Then the chipping away at the territory began. First, it was agreed that the corridor around Jerusalem should be widened, to provide for greater security to Israel's capital. How could anyone doubt the right of a state to protect its capital? Soon Jerusalem came to be announced as the capital *only* of Israel, not to be shared with any future Palestinian state. Then an area just southeast of Jerusalem, where kibbutzim had been destroyed in 1948, was considered a legitimate area for a Jewish settlement. Quickly a large city, Efrat, grew up there. More and more compromises were made and repeatedly Israeli governments failed to stop the very enthusiastic settlement project. Eventually, with Likud in power at most times after 1977, it became government policy to encourage further settlements. Then mortgage rates and other conditions were created to encourage people to move across the Green Line for economic reasons as well as ideological. As a result, the settler community (if you include the areas around Jerusalem) has risen to about half a million.

Occupation of the territories was an inevitable result of the victory and the conquest. Their settlement was not. This was a series of decisions made by various governments due to pressure, first from forces within the National Religious Party (who were usually needed to form coalitions), where radicals ousted the former moderate leadership, and then from the growing settler community itself. They were joined by a very large portion of the *mizraḥi* community. Most of these were not settlers, but the idea of an enlarged and hopefully Arab-free state of Israel was attractive to them. Bearing heavy memories of what they considered oppression both by the Muslims in the lands from which they had come, but resenting even more their treatment by the Ashkenazic and leftist elite during their early years in the country (certainly with much justification), they became a right-wing voting bloc. This was not a statement about their economic views or place in the class structure of Israeli society. On the contrary, a great many of them remained working class and members of the Histadrut labor union. They were a generation ahead of the drift in America of working class voters to the Trumpist right, reacting to what they saw as a snobbish and condescending elite. But because of the strong ethos of Jewish unity that the country needed, their hatred was turned, at least publicly, toward the Palestinians. Their representatives in the Knesset became spokesmen for some of the most horridly anti-Arab stereotyping in the country, often performed in screaming tones and seemingly intended to rile up their base. While the attacks on Arabs in the West Bank over the last few years have been carried out by what are called "hilltop youth," the radical fringe within the religious settler movement, Likud and *mizraḥi* hostility toward Arabs within the country is a powder keg and there are plenty who would be happy to ignite it.

The decline of socialist ideology among secular Israelis went hand in hand with the tremendous growth of the economy, some of which must indeed be credited to the early years of Netanyahu's administration. Israel began to pride itself as "Startup Nation" and significant fortunes were made by people who found their way into the field of high-tech innovation. In those same years, the last two decades of the 20th century, television and other media, in addition to increased travel, also brought Israelis into much closer communication with American society and values. The American Dream of comfortable living in suburbia became very much the Israeli dream as well. Ideology and a sense of collective effort in building the society were cast aside as people, including many who had left the kibbutzim or the labor unions behind, struck out to make their own fortunes. Many of these young people had been through difficult ordeals during their Army Service, especially those who served in the Yom Kippur and Lebanon wars. It felt to them that they deserved a portion of the good life that so many others were attaining.

During its formative years, Israel had seen itself as a highly collectivist society. All had to work together in the creation of a new country. That meant universal army service, which was taken for granted. But it also meant a tremendous emphasis on volunteering, urban youth going out to kibbutz for periods of time, sometimes in the context of the very widespread *naḥal* movement, and other forms of service to the broader community. But as the economy changed, a new ethos of concern for the self, including personal self-improvement, became more the norm. Israelis who completed Army Service created the nearly universal pattern of travel abroad once they were released. Some stayed for a year or more outside the country, often in India, Thailand, or more remote parts of Asia. The next generation discovered the jungles of South America and various islands at what seemed like the far reaches of human civilization. Lots of these, when they came home, brought with them routines of meditation, yoga, massage, and therapeutic skills, dedicated to the betterment of individual lives, their own and those of others. A large service industry sector around the general theme of therapy and psychology, much of it with a "New Age" intonation, became noticeable.

In the same decades that secular society was losing its socialist ideological moorings, the national religious and settler movement was becoming more and more sure of itself, often with the messianic focus as a driver. Some elements within it became quite aggressive in spreading their agenda into the broader population, which seemed indifferent to any sort of devotion to a cause. The rubric was that secular society has an "empty wagon" (or shopping cart) and we, the religious, are here to fill it for them with the beautiful content of Jewish tradition. Of course, this "filling" also brought along with it support of the settler cause, lack of sympathy for the Palestinians, and a broader rejection of "Western values" and even democracy itself, in favor of talmudic and Hasidic worldviews. In many cases, this disdain for the corrupt West, with its addiction to pornography, the breakup of the traditional family, its commitment to LBGTQ rights, etc. was presented as rejection of the world of the *goyim* and a return to true Jewish values. This message, carried in its *mizraḥi* version by the ShaS movement and in its Ashkenazi garb by the *Gar'in Torani* movement, but most successfully by Chabad, has made a significant impact.

This is the place to add a few words about the Chabad movement. This Hasidic sect, rooted in the 18th century, has always been known for being more open than any other to the modern world and to seeking new converts to its cause. In the Soviet era, Chabad *ḥasidim* went to great lengths to keep the candle of Jewish life burning, often at the price of great and sometimes terrible personal sacrifice. When the 6th Chabad rebbe immigrated to New York in 1940, he was already speaking about "Redemption now!" But it was his son-in-law, the 7th and last rebbe of Chabad, who carried his messianism forward. The remarkable messianic movement that emerged within Chabad beginning in the 1980s was parallel to, but quite separate from, that of Gush Emunim. This was a Hasidic messianism rather than a political movement created by messianic dreams. The rebbe offered broad hints that he might be Messiah, or at least was ready to take on that role. The faithful in their enthusiasm went farther and declared him to be the redeemer. Some of them referred to him, rather shockingly, as an incarnation of God Himself.

The messianic movement within Chabad also needs to be seen as the reaction both to the Holocaust and to the victory of 1967. The Chabad rebbe, like all of his colleagues in that role, was unable to explain where the divine hand had been in the days of Auschwitz. He could not accept the harsh judgment offered by the Hungarian *hasidim* that the Holocaust had been a punishment for both Zionism and Reform and their abandonment of God's Torah. That judgment was far too severe for his demeanor or that of his movement. His answer, too, was that these had been the birth pangs of Messiah and now redemption was on its way. Because Chabad had a long tradition of opposition to Zionism, that redemptive process could not be identified with the Israeli state. Instead, it was personified in the rebbe himself.

But the events of 1967 onward pushed the Chabad movement to ever greater and greater acceptance of the Zionist reality. Wanting to reach out to Israelis and other Jews around the world, they could not be seen as rejecting the State of Israel. Today, I am sad to report that large parts of the support received by the farthest right and most racist Israeli political party, that led by Itamar Ben Gvir, comes from Chabad *hasidim*. I cannot believe that this support has nothing to do with the Chabad doctrine, clearly stated in the *Tanya*, its second Bible, that only Jews possess divine souls.

Here we need to look back on the twin Jewish values of *ahavat yisra'el* and *ahavat ha-beriot*, loving Jews and loving humanity. There are many within Chabad who understand the two as a continuum rather than an opposition. I can say this unequivocally of the Chabad rabbi in whose synagogue I *daven* every week, and he is surely not alone in this.[52] There is a large movement within Chabad to reach out to non-Jews through convincing them to observe the seven Noahide commandments. But in Israel, where the openly messianic wing dominates within Chabad, I fear that its embrace of right-wing Zionism has brought forth a deadly mixture of ontologically-based chauvinism and military aggressiveness. Even government ministers, especially those many of these Chabadniks most support, seem to ignore the rules given to the sons of Noah.

This can be seen most clearly in the works of Rabbi Yitzhak Ginsburgh, one of the leading figures within Israeli Chabad. He is a prolific author, one who travels and lectures widely. He is also known as the inspirational leader of the "hilltop youth" described above. For him, the "love of Israel" has everything to do with the essential difference between Jew and Gentile. The latter should not be allowed to live in the Land of Israel unless they meet special requirements that designate them "the righteous of the nations." The Arab population should, in one way or another, be pushed out of the country. But Israel itself, as a secular, democratic state, is also illegitimate. Ginsburg has outlined a whole step-by-step plan for the transformation of Israel into a theocratic monarchy. It is unclear how many of his followers actually go along with his plan in its entirety, but they surely use his teachings as an inspiration for opposition to any sort of Palestinian rights. While he has repeatedly claimed that he is opposed to violence in acting out his ideas, it would be folly to think that those inspired by him take this seriously.[53]

---

[52] To show the complexity of these matters, it is the Chabad *Nusah ha-Ari* prayerbook that replaces the daily 'amidah phrase "For You hear the prayer of Your people Israel" with "For You hear the prayer of every mouth." This clearly seems to imply that God hears the prayers of Gentiles along with those of Jews.

[53] Interestingly, Ginsburgh, Meyer Kahane, and Baruch Goldstein (who murdered Arab worshippers in the Cave of Machpelah) are/were all Ameri-

Parallel to Ginsburgh, but coming out of the Zvi Yehudah Kook school, stands Rabbi Zvi Thau, head of the Har ha-Mor yeshivah, and the other chief influencer among the Israeli religious far right. These are people within the religious Zionist community, still committed to the state, but who have moved toward extreme observance of Jewish practice in various ways. Thau presents himself primarily as a defender of traditional values, especially that of the Jewish family. He is known largely as a fierce crusader against homosexuality and its threat to the family unit. But he is also a spokesman for a much broader rejection of Western values imported to Israel, including that of democracy. He, too, would like to see Israel turn into a full theocracy.

Thau has great influence in some circles within the military. This influence is partly used to enforce separation of men and women and other forms of religious extremism previously unknown in the Armed Forces. But he is also an influence on those who see no place for the Palestinian people in the area between the Jordan River and the sea. This is to become an exclusively Jewish kingdom, where Torah will rule. Secular Israelis will either repent and turn religious or eventually emigrate from the country. This is where Zionist messianism seems to lead.

---

can Jews. Does growing up in the Orthodox Holocaust survivor community in America provide a breeding ground where some people come out with a special hatred of *goyim*?

2025: Where We Stand Today

The severe crisis in relations between Western thinking Jews and the Israeli government did not begin with the reaction to the slaughter of October 7, 2023. It began nine months earlier, in January of that year, with the formation of the most right-wing government in Israel's history. When Binyamin Netanyahu announced that he was forming a government that included both the National Religious Party, which had become a voice for the radical settler movement, and the Jewish Power Party, led by a man who represents Kahanist racism and hatred of Arabs, we knew we were already in big trouble.

Because of the precariousness of coalition party politics, these two party leaders, Bezalel Smotrich and Itamar Ben Gvir, have dominated many of the decisions supposedly undertaken by the Prime Minister. His fear of losing the basis of his coalition (aggravated by fear of his own legal troubles) has caused him to place the fate of Israel, as well as that of the people of Gaza and the West Bank, in their hands.

Shortly after the new government was formed, its justice minister Yariv Levin rushed headlong into a campaign to weaken the Israeli Supreme Court. This was done for a single reason. In the parliamentary system, there is no possibility of checks and balances between the legislative and executive branches of the government. The Prime Minister, by definition, represents the majority power in the Knesset. As a result, the most important brake on the government's absolute control is the judiciary, ultimately the Supreme Court. The court, under the leadership of distinguished jurists over the years, has had the task of representing constitutional restraint when governmental power gets out of hand. Its rulings have by no means been consistently liberal, but it represents a key embodiment of democracy in the Israeli system.

This does not mean that there were no problems within the Israeli judiciary. It should have reflected a broader picture of the diverse Israeli population. Perhaps there was a degree of haughtiness in relation to other parts of the government. Some of that was understandable, given the quality of some voices prominent within the Knesset. But all this was and is remediable without undermining the court's authority.

But here's the scoop. The Israeli right, including those two minority parties alongside Netanyahu's Likud, seeks to annex the West Bank. This has been their dream since 1967. In doing so, they have no intention of giving Palestinian residents there anything like the vote or equal rights. Presumably, they would continue to be governed by military rule, as they have been since 1967. This huge and transformative injustice can only be prevented by the court, which would most likely declare it illegal. Going ahead with it in open defiance of the court would create a constitutional crisis that Netanyahu would like to avoid. Therefore, gutting the power of the court is the only way forward. The campaign against Israel's Attorney General has been part of the same process. It is all designed to lay the groundwork for annexation without empowerment of the Arab population, and possibly toward moves leading to its expulsion.

The very impressive large demonstrations against this move represented the best of Western-looking Israel. It was encouraging to see a significant part of the secular Israeli population, so very self-satisfied and non-ideological in recent years, resisting this antidemocratic effort. It was upsetting, on the other hand, to see how few religious Israelis and how very few *mizrahim* joined in the protest. From their point of view, this was a protest movement of the privileged, wanting to protect their own way of life. The Israeli Palestinians also looked askance at the protest movement, seeing it as designed to protect democracy for Jewish citizens of the state, but not for others. They were not entirely wrong.

This period of protest came to an abrupt end on October 7. The effect of that terrible day, which brought back all the Jewish nightmares of pogrom and Holocaust, sent the entire society into a state of trauma, from which it has not even begun to recover. Israel is still living inside the shudder caused by the events of that day, to a degree that is hard for outsiders to understand. Every Jew in Israel has a sense of "It could have been me or my children who were killed in that terrible way." Open declarations of hatred for all Arabs have been legitimized in a way they never were until now. You hear them from politicians as well as newscasters and interviewees on Israeli news programs all the time. *Ḥayyot adam* is a phrase I heard with some frequency while watching television news over the past couple of years: they are "human animals."

How I wish I could say that this has nothing to do with our tradition! How I wish I could understand it simply as the dehumanization that happens in the course of war, the way American soldiers referred to Vietnamese as *gooks*. But I'd be lying to you—and to myself—if I tried to get away with that. Echoes of ancient tropes cannot be denied. That sense of Jewish superiority implies, or at least makes it easier to accept, the inferiority of others. Once they act against you in seemingly inhuman ways, the trap is set.

The truly awful suffering of the Israeli hostages and the widespread identification with them has allowed Israelis to continue, over these past two years, to see themselves as victims. Victimhood fits Jews so well, like an old coat. We know exactly how to wear it, because we've been doing so for such a long time. The notion that we are victimizers, oppressors, killers on a large scale, is intolerable to us. That's just not who Jews are! Of course not!

Claims to the contrary must be lies, because they completely contradict any experience we have of what it means to be a Jew. We *must* be the victims here! We *need* to be the victims!

What are we to do? We attend protest rallies, but they are usually billed as protests for the hostages. A worthy cause, of course, but one in which we are still the victims. We write and send around petitions, we try to raise our voice of concern over things happening both in Gaza and the West Bank. But the Israeli government pays no attention. It has no interest in what half of Israeli citizenry thinks about this, and even less in listening to the voices of the Jewish diaspora. In fact, disdain for our opposition only strengthens them with their base. "We'll show them!"

Despair over the situation, including the terrible fate of the Palestinian civilians, the suffering of the Israeli hostages and their loved ones, and the government's disregard for any opposition, has led a number of important American Jewish thinkers to declare themselves non- or anti-Zionists. They have given up on the notion of the Jewish State, which they consider to be an intolerable expression of exclusive ethnic nationalism. I understand their point of view, and I put the blame entirely on the Israeli government for having driven them, and many thousands of young Jews along with them, toward that position. But I am not capable of joining them. I am fiercely opposed to everything this awful Israeli government is doing. But it has not yet succeeded in making me reject my belief in the need for, and the potential legitimacy of, a Jewish state—alongside a Palestinian one.

I am neither a politician nor a political scientist. Therefore, I do not claim the ability or feel the obligation to lay out a specific plan for the future of Israel/Palestine. Generally, I am most impressed with the design being put forth by a group called *A Land for All*, which describes a future based on a confederation of two independent states with open rights of residence, travel, and employment between them. (Check out their website.) There is no possibility of peace or long-term survival for Israel unless the Palestinians also have a resolution that restores their pride as a nation as well as political rights to them as individuals. The question, of course, is how we get from here to there. This will require new leadership and the rebirth of vision on both sides. It will also require a process similar to that of South Africa's "Commission on Reconciliation." The worst tragedy of October 7 is that it has set us back, perhaps by decades, in the inevitable march toward that future.

The decision to create a Jewish state brought us back to the realm of history. For 2,000 years, we thought of ourselves as living somewhere in a state of suspended animation. This was *galut*, that long period between destruction and Messiah. That defined our existence. The history of the nations was not our history; we lived by a different calendar.

But Zionism was the decision to step out of that closet, to become an active historical player and take our fate into our own hands. With that came *responsibility*. The success of Zionism, the creation of a Jewish state, increased that responsibility many times over. Not only do we have independence and therefore responsibility for our own behavior, but we also rule over a 20% non-Jewish minority. They have every right to count on us as a people that represents an ancient and noble moral tradition. In many cases we have failed to live up to that.

Once we were successful in the Six Day War and conquered a much larger non-Jewish population, not citizens of our country, our responsibility grew even greater. Yes, there have been many bad actors and awful deeds committed by the other side. We did not inherit a submissive population or one lacking a tradition of violence. That is all true. But there is no *ribbonut*, rule, that comes without *aḥrayut*, responsibility. We cannot push it off onto others.

My concern in this book has not been to resolve the political problem, but rather to address the spiritual/religious one. There is a reading of our beloved tradition that has led the way to dangerous and unacceptable moral views. There is a strain of superiority and condescension toward others that can find support by quoting lots of texts from within the corpus that constitutes Judaism, from biblical down to Hasidic times. The mystical and Hasidic tradition, which I happen to love for other reasons, is particularly rife with these. In Judaism as it thrives in the Land of Israel, they are particularly close to the surface, having a frightening amount of influence. Gershom Scholem, the father of modern critical study of Kabbalah, warned many years ago, at the conclusion of his book *Major Trends in Jewish Mysticism*, that the return of Jews to the Land of Israel would bring about a revival of the mystical spirit, including all its glory and all its dangers. Right now, those dangers loom very large.

Response

Remember, I believe that Judaism is a *derekh in avoyde*, a path of service. What does it mean to serve Y-H-W-H? In my understanding, that means serving humanity, the natural (or "created") world, and the earth itself, all the beings, places, and moments where Y-H-W-H is to be found. It is a life of *awareness* and *response*, cultivating a sense of wonder and living in response to it. We need to understand this "service" in a most expansive way. "Broadening the boundaries of the holy" is what the Hasidic masters used to call it. If "G-O-D" does not work for you, I have no argument with you. You may render Y-H-W-H as "Being," "Existence," or "the Breath of Life." If you are a devotional type, like I am, you may choose to express that service through ritual acts and words of prayer. If you do not feel a need for or an attraction to these, but approach your life as an opportunity to serve, you are still living in response to the covenant, our encounter at the foot of Mount Sinai.

The memory of Sinai (again, I am not speaking in the language of historical claim) transformed us from a natural people to a community of faith that together walks a spiritual path. Yes, we see ourselves as children of Abraham, who went to the Land of Israel in response to what he understood as a divine call. Our claim to that land is a very ancient one, a claim that we never abandoned. But we are also the people of Moses, who splashed that blood over us and declared us as belonging to Y-H-W-H in a particular way. There we declared ourselves a kingdom of priests, ready to serve. From that moment, we heard ourselves saying: "The land and all that fills it **belongs to Y-H-W-H** (Ps. 24:1)." It belongs to God; none of it belongs to us. Especially not anything called the "Holy Land."

"You can't have it both ways!" you might say. But we *must* have it both ways. That is who we are. Hold onto this truth, Scripture tells us, *but don't let go of that one, either* (Ecc. 7:18). Much of Judaism may be seen as constructed around that verse. We are a natural people, one with natural needs. Security is right at the top of that list. But we are also a people committed to a *supernatural* perception of reality, one that sees the miraculous in every moment and celebrates its presence, having vowed to live in response to it. Our collective *priesthood* is one of witnessing that truth to the world.

I believe we must move forward holding on to both of these truths. I welcome Jews who think of themselves as secular to broaden the understanding of our covenant and to see it as a covenant of commitment to life, earth, or humanity, rather than to "God." But I do not accept the abandonment of that covenant or its universality. It is a commitment made *by* the Jewish people, but it is not just a commitment *to* the Jewish people. The whole point of it is to reach beyond our own selves and self-interests, toward a universal truth.

I therefore oppose the sort of Zionism that wants to "solve the Jewish problem" by the "normalization" of the Jewish people, taking us in an exclusively national direction. The prophet Samuel already warned us against trying to be "like all the other nations" (I Sam. 8) when we first wanted to proclaim a king, making us into a defined political entity. Today, certainly, it will not succeed. Perhaps that is what we are seeing unfold before our eyes. The sense of being an *am segulah*, a people with a special character and mission, is so deeply ingrained within us that it does not depart, even in our attempt to secularize. Instead, as we have seen, it can turn into something ugly.

I affirm our people's right to have returned to our ancient homeland. I do not believe it to be ours by divine promise, since

I do not know a God who makes such promises. Our right to return there is due to our rich history there in ancient times and our ongoing loyalty to memory of it, and spiritual ties to it, over countless generations. Our claim to that return was legitimate and did not require the Palestinian people's permission. But to take it all, rather than to share it, is not the way this people is supposed to act. Anyone who begins the study of Talmud learns this lesson. "Two people are holding on to a garment. One says, 'It's all mine' and the other says, 'It's all mine.'" Ultimately, there is nothing to do but divide it. The land of Israel is not the baby in the judgment of Solomon. We do not need to engage in a life-and-death contest to see who loves it more. A land *can* be divided.

Yes, some of you will tell me. We tried. We were willing. Remember Oslo, remember Olmert. It was the Palestinians who were unwilling to compromise. They never had a leadership courageous enough to take that plunge. You are not entirely wrong. But remember: Yitshak Rabin was assassinated for his willingness to compromise, and not by a Palestinian. It is the people who agitated for that assassination and those who stood by quietly but benefited from it, who are now running the country. Remember also how hard Israel has tried, especially in the Netanyahu era, to weaken that Palestinian leadership. We were afraid of a strong, respected, and flexible Palestinian leadership. We kept Marwan Bargouti, the most likely such leader, in jail. We even allowed all those millions of dollars to go to Hamas, via Qatar, precisely in order to counter and weaken the Palestinian authority.

I am not a Jew who gives easy credence to the traditional notion of Particular Providence, the idea that God willfully controls history and chooses the fate of either nations or individuals. The Holocaust made that impossible for me, as did various events of my own life. But I cannot help but look upon our history over the course of the past century as calling forth a sense that some mysterious meaning is to be seen within it, which one may choose to depict as a divine hand. The period after the Second World War witnessed the breakup of all the great colonial empires, including those of the British, the French, the Dutch, and the Portuguese. Ultimately, this came to include the Soviet empire as well. New nations were emerging and old hostilities that had been covered over by colonial rule suddenly came bubbling to the surface, revealing ancient rivalries and competition for living space. Biafra. Rwanda. Bosnia. Kosovo. Sri Lanka. The list could go on.

At that very moment (a year after the liberation and partition of India, the largest of all colonies) this ancient holy people, having tried so hard to shed that mantle of holiness and step back into history, stakes its claim and proclaims a state. It is confronted by the most intractable of all these conflicts, that of Israelis and Palestinians, still unresolved 70 years later, making daily headlines across the world.

Can this be coincidence? Even if you think it is, can we find meaning in it? I believe that we and our tradition are being put to a test, the greatest in all our long history. We rose from the ashes of the Holocaust like a brand plucked from the fire. Amazingly, with a third of us dead and the rest of us still utterly stunned by the blow, we were given—again, by God or by history—an opportunity for rebirth. We took hold of it and created a reborn Jewish society, one with a rich culture, a successful economy, and all the rest.

And yet, perhaps we are still failing the test. We, bearing with us our ancient claim to a great moral legacy, were placed in the midst of this most difficult of all intergroup conflicts. Would we resolve it with justice? Would we allow Nathan the Prophet (he of "the poor man's lamb"), along with Isaiah and Amos, to help shape our conduct? Or would we just revere them as witness to the "greatness of Israel's heritage," while still proclaiming, "It's all mine!" and ignoring their message? We were given this opportunity to show the world how to resolve such conflicts; that's why we were placed in the middle of this one. But we have failed quite miserably at that task.

What are we politically impotent bystanders, especially Jews living outside of Israel, supposed to do about it? I will admit that the verses spoken about Koraḥ in the Book of Numbers come to mind: "Separate yourselves from those wicked people who are about to be destroyed!" Stand back and let the calamity they have brought on themselves happen! But, of course, I am far from able to even imagine taking such a course. I am not ready, unlike some others, to proclaim a new diasporist Judaism, presumably leaving Israel to its fate. Nor are most diaspora Jews. The calamity of Israel's conduct in these years will ultimately fall on the people of Israel, not just the government. We are deeply tied to Israel, including bonds of love, family, dear friendships, and all we have gained from the incredibly rich and diverse cultural creativity that exists there. While I firmly believe that the Jewish people needs two creative centers, rather than one (*Babylon and Jerusalem*, in the words of scholar and Hebraist Simon Rawidowicz), our center here in Babylon cannot thrive without the other pole. We are nourished by the deep-rootedness in Jewish living found in Israel, the renewed Hebrew language, and the great literary, artistic, and scholarly creativity that takes place there. But because of what I see happening in Israel these days, I believe more than ever that they cannot exist without us, either. The "Survive at all cost!" and "Your life comes first!" slogans ring so loudly because of Israel's situation (yes, partially self-created, but only partially so) that moral clarity has gotten lost, and with it the reason for our existence over all these millennia tends to get forgotten.

It is our job to help provide that moral clarity. We have been living and thinking about Jewish life in the modern world much longer than Israel has. Because we live in such a multicultural environment, we understand how to learn from others and share with them of our tradition, without feeling threatened by that process. Israelis traditionally detest being preached at by Jews from the Diaspora, but here we are in such deep water that we have to do so without hesitation. A Judaism defined by a defensive turning inward is not what Israel needs, but lately it seems to be getting little else.

I spend half my life in Israel these days; I do so partly to know Israel from the inside. I am not an Israeli citizen, but I am a Jew who feels quite fully at home there. As I said in the introduction, the "we" I often use in this book means that I identify with Israel, a project collectively created by the Jewish people all over the world. We in the Diaspora certainly cannot tell Israelis what to do, but we can remind them of what we think are the essential truths and values of being Jewish in an open and free society. This will be quite different from the message they get from those forces in Israel who are constantly seeking to convince them to "repent" and become *baʿaley teshuvah*, returnees to the Orthodox path.

Let me say a few final words about those truths. There are four principles that I call *Yesodot ha-Torah*, the fundaments of our teaching. Two of them are the first two of the 10 Commandments and the other two are those (see chapter two above) Rabbi Akiva and Ben Azzai each declared to be the most basic principle of Torah. We therefore come out with the following list:

> I am Y-H-W-H your God, who brought you forth from the Land of Egypt, the house of bondage.
>
> Have no other gods alongside Me. Do not bow down to them and do not serve them.
>
> Love your neighbor as yourself.

> Every person, male and female, is made in the image of God.

This is not an arbitrary list. It comes directly out of the tradition, not from an attempt to impose "Western values" on it. The mystical tradition says that all positive commandments in the Torah derive from the first of the Ten Commandments and all negative commandments or prohibitions derive from the second.[54] The Zohar[55] says in one place that all the other 611 Commandments are to serve as "counsels," or advice, in helping us to fulfill these two, a passage widely quoted in Hasidic sources. The competing declarations by two of our most important early sages as to what constitutes the most basic rule of Torah should actually stand side-by-side. "Love your neighbor" when that neighbor is able to receive your love and respond to it. But even your unlovable neighbor—and we Jews have had plenty of those—is the living image of God, just as you are, and you must treat them that way.

Talmudic tradition ascribes special status to the first two commandments as the only ones "heard from the divine mouth," directly from God.[56] I agree with Maimonides in not believing that God has a mouth, at least as we imagine one. If God has no mouth, the commandments cannot quite be *spoken* as we understand that term. These two utterances do not have to be understood as verbal. The realization of Y-H-W-H—*however you choose to translate it*—makes a person free. The first of the Ten Commandments is not just about our own liberation from Egypt, but about everyone's liberation and right of every person

---

[54] Tikkuney Zohar 20, 63b-64a. But see also Maimonides' *Sefer ha-Mitsvot*, first commandment. The claim of the Tikkunim is carried further in interesting ways by *Degel Maḥaneh Ephraim, Tsav*.
[55] 2:82b.
[56] Makkot 24a.

to be free from all that binds us or narrows our vision. The Hasidic masters regularly read *mitsrayim*, "Egypt" in this verse as *meytsarim*, the narrow straits, anything from which we need to be liberated. Because Y-H-W-H is present within each human soul, the right to freedom belongs to every human being. The second commandment means that nothing compares to that truth; nothing should stand alongside it as a subject of worship or an object of value. It warns us away, not just from the molten images of antiquity, but from all the idols we worship, even today. I do not need to list them here; they are too well known to us all.

That is our essential message, both to ourselves and to the world. If we allow loyalty to any Israeli government to trump any of these (or, indeed, to become a nationalist idolatry), we are lost. We exist as a people, ever since Sinai, to bear witness to these truths. That witness, of course, is primarily one of deeds, not of words. Our return to the world of history, politics, and governance was an opportunity to increase that witness, to "Magnify and Sanctify" the great name Y-H-W-H throughout God's created world. We started off well, but got badly diverted—by insecurity, by temptation, and by that old bugaboo of valuing our own humanity just a little bit more than that of others.

It is time to get back on track. Everything depends on it. We need to reclaim our tradition, to offer a robust vision of Judaism that stands firmly on these four values, applied in their fullest and most universal way. The "we" in this call includes two groups who bear significant responsibility for the calamity that has come upon us. One of those groups is the bulk of American Jewry, who have passively slid into a weak form of Jewish identity, one consisting of bagels and lox and few garbled Yiddish words. For many, a good bit of Larry David-style self-loathing is thrown into the mix. We American Jews have gotten comfortable with the notion that the real center of action is elsewhere, that it is Israel that is shaping the Jewish future. Prime Minister Netanyahu tells us that whenever he has a chance, and we let him.

We now have seen that we cannot leave the fate of our Jewish legacy in Israel's hands. The abysmal quality of Israeli political life and many of those who lead it must shock us into awakening. Things being done in the name of the Jewish people, including both the intentional starvation of a civilian population in Gaza and the theft and murder that go on daily on the West Bank, need to shake us out of our passivity. We need to engage in an active campaign—I called it a "crusade" in the introduction to this book—to take the tradition back. That includes loudly and publicly denouncing the desecration of God's name and that of the Jewish people by the current Israeli government.

Our natural allies in this effort are the so-called "secular" Israelis, those who bravely rally against the war, those who stood up for democracy in huge numbers before the calamity of October 7. Many of these are people of values, motivated by a great concern for human decency and justice. A lot of them have been pushed rightward by the October 7 massacre, just as the Israeli left was vitiated by the second intifada some 20 years ago, a blow from which it never recovered.

These Jews are already products of two or three generations of indifference to Judaism, including active hostility to its Orthodox form. Some of their grandparents thought they were leaving "Jewish" behind and exchanging it for a new identity as "Israeli." They are now learning, partly through the terrible legacy of October 7 and its ongoing trauma, that this transformation is neither so simple nor so complete as they had thought. On October 8, the word "pogrom" re-entered the vocabulary of many Israelis, causing a great national collective shudder, a realization that Jewish history did not end in 1948.

If you ask this population the ideological question "Are you secular or religious?" they will answer, "Secular," quite emphatically. If you ask, "Do you believe in God?" you will get a mix, with many saying "No" partly because they resent the question. But if you ask about the markers of Jewish life, from a mezuzah on their door to whether they light Hanukkah candles, or have a Passover Seder, or even fast on Yom Kippur, the numbers will be quite different. For many Israelis, there is a desire to reclaim something of Judaism without being pushed into being "religious," which to them means Orthodox. Only a very small number have been attracted to the non-Orthodox synagogue movements that have tried to root themselves in Israel. Synagogues do not seem to be the way Israelis want to express either their Jewish identity or their spiritual search. But that does not mean that either of these is lacking.

This part of Israeli society needs to reclaim Judaism as its own, to be convinced to take responsibility, not only for the future political direction of their country, but for the use and misuse of Judaism and its symbolic language in its public arena. The old bargain of allowing the ultra-religious to define the tradition in the most rigid of ways, so that we can proclaim it ridiculous and justify our abandonment of it, no longer works. The demonstrators of 2023 notably took the Israeli flag back, refusing to let it belong to the right wing alone. They need to do the same for the language of Judaism itself and to themselves define what it stands for. The tools of ancient religious tropes and symbols are so powerful that they cannot be left in the hands of those who interpret them in the narrowest and most exclusivist ways. They need to be taken back.

The onetime distinction between Judaism of the West, that cleaned-up version called "mainstream," and the pre-modern forms of Judaism that survived in the East, has broken down over the past several decades. The rekindled interest in Kabbalah and Hasidism has had a great role in that, one in which I have been an active participant. This interest is the result of much broader intellectual and spiritual currents in the Western world, leading to the new interest in Eastern and esoteric spirituality since the 1960s. That interest does not seem to have abated and the continuing revival of both Kabbalah and Neo-Hasidism (they are quite distinct from one another) is very much a part of it. It is interesting to note that the Bergs, creators of the once highly popular Kabbalah Centers, were happy to teach this wisdom to non-Jews and to women, crossing lines that had been strictly guarded in previous generations. I once thought this to be simply a "commercial" decision, but I was wrong. The mentor behind their movement, the Kabbalist Yehudah Leib Ashlag (1886–1954), who was himself quite a modern figure, a socialist and universalist, supported such extended outreach.

Neo-Hasidism has been around since the 1920s. It disappeared because of the Holocaust, was resurrected by two charismatic rabbis in the 1960s, Shlomo Carlebach and Zalman Schachter, and has now grown to hold a significant place on the Jewish spiritual stage. It takes many forms and it crosses denominational lines. Its original masters, Martin Buber and Hillel Zeitlin, took pains to universalize Hasidic teachings as they passed them on to new generations of readers. So too my teacher Abraham Joshua Heschel, who came out of the Hasidic milieu but became a leader in interfaith conversation, conducted himself with full respect for the Other. What the Hasidic sources said about the souls of Israel was taken by these teachers to apply to all human souls. Carlebach (sometimes) and Schachter were of the same spirit, and all the non-Orthodox versions of Neo-Hasidism now take that universalization for granted. But because of the outreach to newcomers within two existing old-time Hasidic communities, Chabad and Braslav, the Neo-Hasidism that is taking shape within Orthodoxy is at much greater risk. The dynamic energy of Hasidism, combined with the nationalist and "pioneering" spirit felt by the most radical of West Bank settlers, is precisely the most dangerous of powder kegs, as described above in discussing the influence of Rabbi Yitsḥak Ginsburgh and others like him.

The other and much larger reason why the old "mainstream" has melted away is the acceptance of the national element within Judaism by all elements within the Diaspora community, including Reform Judaism, where it was long resisted. All agree that it is no longer possible or even desirable to go back to the pre-1930s attempt to define Judaism simply as a religion, in the Protestant sense. We Jews are a people, as we have been since that first chapter of Exodus, and that means that we are linked to one another both across generations and across the seas. Because travel has been made so much easier in recent decades, countless American Jews have discovered Israeli relatives or have created friendships with Israeli families. That is all a very positive development. We need to make use of it in our campaign to recover Judaism from the hands of those who read it in narrowly exclusive, and sometimes downright racist, ways.

I bring these two together, the recovery of Jewish spirituality and the international quality of the Jewish people, because I think they together offer great potential. I have devoted most of my life to recovering or re-creating what I call a *Judaism for Seekers*, people who have more questions than answers, but long to find a sense of deeper meaning in their lives, and to do so through Judaism. There is a vast number of such seekers on both sides of the Israel/Diaspora divide. We need to open a doorway to Judaism for them in a way that it has never been opened before. The spiritual blandness of liberal Judaism in America and the sharp Orthodox/secular divide in Israel have kept them away. Over the past several decades, we have seen tens, perhaps hundreds, of thousands of American Jews turning to the religions of the Far East for spiritual sustenance and growth, believing that Judaism had nothing to offer them, or was closed to them because they didn't "know enough." We all know the jokes about the Tibetan lama Irving and his mother Mrs. Goldberg. At the same time, we've seen many thousands of Israelis, returning from that journey in their post-army years, and trying to find at home an equivalent to the deep and impressive spirituality they witnessed and experienced in the Far East or in the jungles of South America. Some create yoga studios in Tel Aviv; others turn to Braslav. But there are many who would like to find another road into Judaism, one that understands what they mean by seeking and is not judgmental about issues of personal lifestyle. The use of psychedelics, including ayahuasca, is very widespread among Israeli seekers. A new Jewish spirituality will have to include careful embrace of psychedelic elements.

This move toward a new exploration of Judaism has to be strong in its meditative, intellectual, and musical creativity. It should not push hard on religious observance, because that is precisely the "button" that so-called secular Israelis fear most. There is a large movement in Israel toward what is called *hadatah*, the smiley-faced imposition of religious behavior on the secular public. We need to show that we are very far from that—precisely, an alternative to it. We need to make it clear constantly that our role is twofold: the personal spiritual growth of the seeker and the creation of an Israeli Jewish public that will indeed *save Judaism*, taking responsibility to re-steer its course.

Israel has long described itself as a Jewish and democratic state. The "and" in that sentence points to a tension between those two. Indeed, that tension has long been recognized. It is assumed that democracy is a secular value, and therefore primarily supported by the secular segment of the population. "Jewish" is to be defined in halakhic and other sorts of traditional categories, and will necessarily stand in contrast to "democratic." Many Israelis are rightly concerned with the preservation of democracy in their country. I am concerned, however, with the rehabilitation of the "Jewish" part of that equation. I hope Israel will strive toward being a *Democratic Jewish State*, dropping the "and." It is true, of course, that "democracy" is nowhere mentioned in the Torah. It is a value of Greek rather than Hebrew origin. As I have shown, however, freedom is very much a biblical value, according to the first of the 10 Commandments. An awful lot can be done with that in terms of defining what it means to be a freedom-loving Jewish state, one that embraces freedom for all its citizens. The value of human creation in the divine image also gives us a notion of equality of all people. Freedom and equality go a long way in creating the democratic part of a Democratic Jewish State.

I am suggesting that a shared community of religious seekers, North Americans and Israelis, needs to serve as a bridge to help awaken both of their wider communities to the dangers and the great potential of the moment. We need to be advocates for such an Israel and for such a set of values throughout the Jewish people. This effort needs to be a joint and equally balanced Diaspora/Israeli one. Here I return to an idea mentioned briefly above, that of a dual centered Jewish community, as described in Rawidowicz's *Babylon and Jerusalem*. For too long, we have let the Israeli government and the Zionist establishment get away with proclaiming Israel alone as the center of Jewish life. American Jewish philanthropists created a vast program called Birthright, sending American Jews for a summer in Israel to reinforce their Jewish identity. In a complementary fashion, many non-Orthodox movements in North American Jewry have established similar programs to bring young Israelis to the US to experience Judaism in its many forms in the Diaspora. They live with American families, are welcomed into local congregations, and have the opportunity to see Judaism through a different lens. They also serve as ambassadors from Israel, sharing their life experiences with their peers and their host community, giving Americans a personal Israeli perspective for a few months, sometimes more. It's a wonderful way for Jewish Israeli and Jewish American youth to connect and learn from each other.

There is a whole new genre of Jewish musical creativity happening in America, quite different from Israeli music. Jewish Rock Radio promotes itself as the voice of Jewish Rock—not Israeli or American. Just Jewish. Music is a wonderful way of bringing young people from these two cultures together on a mutual level. We need to realize that we as American Jews have something to offer our Israeli friends. American Jewry is not an "empty wagon," waiting to be filled with Israeli content. The Israeli seeker has much to learn from approaches to Judaism that have been birthed here, as well as vice versa.

How do we go about this great project of reclamation? I should say at the outset that I am an "ideas person," not a community organizer. But I have had a role in the creation of several important projects in the recent history of American Jewish life. I also see to it that all my books appear in Israel in Hebrew translation, because I care very much about influencing the Israeli public as well as the American Jewish one. We will need a group of dedicated Jewish leaders, including foundations, who will make this project their own. I suggest a series of major conferences, involving both Americans and Israelis, to speak openly and share ideas, including news of already existing efforts that reassert strongly the image of a forward-looking and universalist Judaism. The project should not be identified with any particular denomination or organization, but it should welcome input from a great variety of them. This should include the progressive edge of Orthodoxy, best represented right now by a group called *Smol Emuni*, the faithful left, coming out of Israel, but having an impact here as well. Educational efforts, on both sides of the ocean but also joint, including use of Zoom, will need to be designed, both for adults and for youth. Programs for post-army Israeli young people to come to the US for six months or a year to participate in creative corners of American Jewish life, not just to serve as armed guards at our synagogues and Jewish Centers, might be a good idea.

Of course, such an effort will require major funding. I would suggest that younger family members of some of the major foundations might play an important role here. This should also be an opportunity to welcome back into the Jewish community the very large number of young Jews who have turned away from Israel in disgust. We have been foolish in driving them away by proclaiming that their views are not to be heard in any Jewish communal context. Nothing could be more self-destructive of a minority community seeking a future than driving away some of its most impassioned and serious potential leaders! Bring them back to talk about how we change the face of Israel and the face of Judaism that has been so maligned by its government's actions. I believe that many of them will welcome the opportunity.

This crusade will face some serious opposition. Neither AIPAC nor the Jewish Agency will be very happy about it. They are still committed to the old model of Israel at the center, and the Diaspora to serve as a cheering section for whatever its government and voters decide to do. We have seen that lead only to calamity and we need to stand up against it. Rabbis and synagogues across the board should be very supportive of this effort and should be organized in commitment to it. Again, there will be opposition by board members committed to a different vision, and we will have to work on local as well as national/international levels to sort that out. I hate to say it, but I fear the actions of the current Israeli regime will be our best ally in displaying how impossible it is to go on as we have until now.

There is another source of funding possible for this project of reclaiming Judaism. It is time for a great "tax revolt" in the American Jewish community. Leadership of that community, the body called "Organized Jewry" lies in the Federation system. Since the early years of the Jewish State, contributions to what were once called Jewish charities, both local and international, have been united under the network of local Jewish

Federations. The donor gives a single gift and the Federation leadership (professionals and the biggest givers) decide how it is to be divided. Around half, sometimes more, regularly goes to Israel. This includes some government-run programs, the Jewish Agency, the Jewish National Fund, and various specific projects that the community has undertaken. These days, a great deal of this money goes to causes which many donors would oppose, if they knew about them. The Israeli government still does not treat non-Orthodox Judaism equally and massively supports young men in draft-avoiding *yeshivot*, to the disgust of most Israelis. JNF acquires and prepares land for settlement in the West Bank. The Jewish Agency is now increasingly dominated by right-wing ideologues and its educational and other priorities will reflect that.[57] It is time for American Jews, the majority of whom are still on the liberal side, to refuse to give, to demand that local needs and Israel funding once again be separated. That would "liberate" a great deal of money for a project like this, as well as for the many great projects supported by the New Israel Fund.[58] Younger generation offspring of those family foundations that now dominate Jewish giving should be most interested in this sort of appeal. We need to find ways to reach out to them.

Stepping back and taking a more wide-angle view of what is happening will also be helpful. *Shivat Tsiyyon*, the return of a large part of the Jewish people to the Land of Israel, created an opportunity for the emergence of a new third era Judaism,

---

[57] The Agency's budget depends on an election within the Zionist movement in many countries, US obviously being the largest. The Orthodox and right-wing Zionist bloc has recently won that election, through a combination of intense campaigning and possible shenanigans. They will determine how a billion dollars of communal funds are spent each year.

[58] The New Israel Fund, established in 1979, has served as a lifeline for support of justice, equality, and democratic values in the Jewish State. Contributions may be given to the fund itself or earmarked for a great variety of worthwhile projects. See their website for details.

one that would mirror neither Israelite religion of biblical times nor that of the long and difficult *galut*. This should have been a Judaism created in and celebrating freedom—the rebirth of an ancient people, proud of its traditions and moral heritage, in a land it had never ceased to love. Instead, the nightmares of the Holocaust and the threats of "We will push you into the sea!" by Arab leaders in Israel's early years (still echoing in Hamas propaganda) created a Judaism of a very different sort, marked by fear of others, defensiveness, and exclusivism. As I have shown, these elements were part of the tradition for a long time, caused and aggravated by the very real oppression Jews suffered for so many centuries. But in an era of freedom and responsibility, we cannot afford for Judaism to remain shackled by those elements. That First Commandment, about taking you out of the House of Bondage, needs to help take that House of Bondage *out of us* as well. Only in doing that will we be able to once again set forth a Judaism that is about loving our neighbor and considering every human being as a living image of Y-H-W-H.

A final word also about setting what is happening to Judaism in a broader context. Because we Jews are both a people and religious community, this has to be seen through two lenses. A burst in religiously inspired nationalism can be seen in many places these days. Modi's India is the most prominent example, but the right-wing Catholic trend in Poland, Bolsonaro's support among evangelicals in Brazil, and Christian Nationalism in the United States are all part of the pattern. One may see both Putin and Trump as part of this phenomenon. While neither is a particularly religious man himself, they both make ready use of religion's popularity to advance and justify their hunger for power. Putin and Modi's denunciations of the "degenerate" West, including much focus on homosexuality, echo Rabbi Thau's version of what is called *HaRDaL* Judaism, roughly to be translated "Extremist Religious Nationalism."

In some of those other cases, too, ancient biases and stereotypes are being brought forth to strengthen the cause. Witness attacks on mosques and Muslims in India, on the Yazidis by Muslims in ISIS, on the Rohinga by Buddhists in Myanmar. Jews have much to fear from such a move if it should happen in Russia or on the American right. The last thing we should be doing is imitating it.

We are also not the only ones among the world's religions to have a problem with exclusivity and disdain for outsiders. It is fair to say that the greatest sin of religions in our world's history is the indifference they have shown for the lives of the heathen, the unsaved, the unbelievers. Many Christians realized this only when they were forced to stare the Holocaust in the face and to ask about the Christian role in allowing it to happen. One may see Vatican II's *Nostra Estate* as an attempt to deal with that and atone for that. There are still forces within the Church that have not accepted it. In other Christian quarters, there are still many who care about the lives of non-Christians only as potential converts. Within Islam, a mighty struggle is going on between ISIS-like forces and peace-loving moderates. The latter are often accused of being "too Western." Sound familiar?

As long as our own very real victimhood protected us from moral responsibility, what we thought about others didn't make much difference. But now it makes *all* the difference. Our problem is ours alone, and it is vital and urgent that we set it right. No amount of "look-over-there"ism will save us from that task.

That is the *avoyde*: the service, the devotion, and the work. Let's get to it. We cannot let Judaism, as a voice of moral conscience, be buried under the rubble of Gaza.

*****

Our teacher R. Hillel Zeitlin, martyr of the Warsaw ghetto, made a habit of adding his address at the end of his many books and essays, saying, "If you're interested in joining me, drop by and we'll chat."

If you are moved by the call of this volume, and especially if you are one who has the influence, means, or skills to help make this crusade happen, drop me a line at agnh2025@gmail.com.

Acknowledgments

I have shared the draft of this book with a number of friends to solicit their comments. I am most grateful to Arnold Eisen, Michael Fishbane, Ebn Leader, Michael Marmur, Ariel Mayse, Tomer Persico, Ariel Pollak, Joseph Reimer, Or Rose, and publisher Larry Yudelson for helping to improve this quickly-written manuscript. Responsibility for all that is said here remains, of course, entirely my own.

In this non-academic book, I have not used footnotes to cite the work of scholars whose writings have obviously influenced my thinking over the years. I here acknowledge all of them collectively and apologize to any one of them who feels that they should have been specifically cited.

Finally, a word to and about Peter Beinart. I had already written (and titled) this book before I had a chance to see his *Being Jewish After Gaza*. Beinart and I have serious political differences. I still believe in the need for and potential legitimacy of a Jewish State, while he does not. But I have profound respect for his integrity and courage. Although our conclusions differ, we are moved by many of the same sensibilities. Beinart has become the *kaporeh hindl*, the scapegoat, for all the rest of us, saving us from the near excommunication that he has suffered. For this I feel I owe him a debt of gratitude.

Recent books from *Ben Yehuda Press*

Judaism Disrupted: A Spiritual Manifesto for the 21st Century by Rabbi Michael Strassfeld. "I can't remember the last time I felt pulled to underline a book constantly as I was reading it, but *Judaism Disrupted* is exactly that intellectual, spiritual and personal adventure. You will find yourself nodding, wrestling, and hoping to hold on to so many of its ideas and challenges. Rabbi Strassfeld reframes a Torah that demands breakage, reimagination, and ownership."
—Abigail Pogrebin, author, *My Jewish Year; 18 Holidays, One Wondering Jew*

The Way of Torah and the Path of Dharma: Intersections between Judaism and the Religions of India by Rabbi Daniel Polish. "A whirlwind religious tourist visit to the diversity of Indian religions: Sikh, Jain, Buddhist, and Hindu, led by an experienced congregational rabbi with much experience in interfaith and in teaching world religions."
—Rabbi Alan Brill, author, *Rabbi on the Ganges: A Jewish Hindu-Encounter*

Liberating Your Passover Seder: An Anthology Beyond The Freedom Seder. Edited by Rabbi Arthur O. Waskow and Rabbi Phyllis O. Berman. This volume tells the history of the Freedom Seder and retells the origin of subsequent new haggadahs, including those focusing on Jewish-Palestinian reconciliation, environmental concerns, feminist and LGBT struggles, and the Covid-19 pandemic of 2020.

Duets on Psalms: Drawing New Meaning from Ancient Words by Rabbis Elie Spitz & Jack Riemer. "Two of Judaism's most inspirational teachers, offer a lifetime of insights on the Bible's most inspired book." — Rabbi Joseph Telushkin, author of *Jewish Literacy* "This illuminating work is a literary journey filled with faith, wisdom, hope, healing, meaning and inspiration."
—Rabbi Naomi Levy, author, *Einstein and the Rabbi*

Weaving Prayer: An Analytical and Spiritual Commentary on the Jewish Prayer Book by Rabbi Jeffrey Hoffman. "This engaging and erudite volume transforms the prayer experience. Not only is it of considerable intellectual interest to learn the history of prayers—how, when, and why they were composed—but this new knowledge will significantly help a person pray with intention (kavvanah). I plan to keep this volume right next to my siddur."
—Rabbi Judith Hauptman, author, *Rereading the Rabbis: A Woman's Voice*

Renew Our Hearts: A Siddur for Shabbat Day edited by Rabbi Rachel Barenblat. From the creator of *The Velveteen Rabbi's Haggadah*, a new siddur for the day of Shabbat. *Renew Our Hearts* balances tradition with innovation, featuring liturgy for morning (*Shacharit* and a renewing approach to *Musaf*), the afternoon (*Mincha*), and evening (*Ma'ariv* and *Havdalah*), along with curated works of poetry, art and new liturgies from across the breadth of Jewish spiritual life. Every word of Hebrew is paired with transliteration and with clear, pray-able English translation.

Forty Arguments for the Sake of Heaven: Why the Most Vital Controversies in Jewish Intellectual History Still Matter by Rabbi Shmuly Yanklowitz. Hillel vs. Shammai, Ayn Rand vs. Karl Marx, Tamar Ross vs. Judith Plaskow... but also Abraham vs. God, and God vs. the angels! Movements debate each other: Reform versus Orthodoxy, one- two- and zero-state solutions to the Israeli-Palestinian conflict, gun rights versus gun control in the United States. Rabbi Yanklowitz presents difficult and often heated disagreements with fairness and empathy, helping us consider our own truths in a pluralistic Jewish landscape.

Recent books from *Ben Yehuda Press*

Reaching for Comfort: What I Saw, What I Learned, and How I Blew it Training as a Pastoral Counselor by Sherri Mandell. In 2004, Sherri Mandell won the National Jewish Book award for *The Blessing of the Broken Heart*, which told of her grief and initial mourning after her 13-year-old son Koby was brutally murdered. Years later, with her pain still undiminished, Sherri trains to help others as a pioneering pastoral counselor in Israeli hospitals. "What a blessing to witness Mandell's and her patients' resilience!" —Rabbi Dayle Friedman, editor, *Jewish Pastoral Care: A Practical Guide from Traditional and Contemporary Sources*

Heroes with Chutzpah: 101 True Tales of Jewish Trailblazers, Changemakers & Rebels by Rabbi Deborah Bodin Cohen and Rabbi Kerry Olitzky. Readers ages 8 to 14 will meet Jewish changemakers from the recent past and present, who challenged the status quo in the arts, sciences, social justice, sports and politics, from David Ben-Gurion and Jonas Salk to Sarah Silverman and Douglas Emhoff. "Simply stunning. You would want this book on your coffee table, though the stories will take the express lane to your soul." —Rabbi Jeff Salkin

Just Jewish: How to Engage Millennials and Build a Vibrant Jewish Future by Rabbi Dan Horwitz. Drawing on his experience launching The Well, an inclusive Jewish community for young adults in Metro Detroit, Rabbi Horwitz shares proven techniques ready to be adopted by the Jewish world's myriad organizations, touching on everything from branding to fundraising to programmatic approaches to relationship development, and more. "This book will shape the conversation as to how we think about the Jewish future."
—Rabbi Elliot Cosgrove, editor, *Jewish Theology in Our Time*.

Put Your Money Where Your Soul Is: Jewish Wisdom to Transform Your Investments for Good by Rabbi Jacob Siegel. "An intellectual delight. It offers a cornucopia of good ideas, institutions, and advisers. These can ease the transition for institutions and individuals from pure profit nature investing to deploying one's capital to repair the world, lift up the poor, and aid the needy and vulnerable. The sources alone—ranging from the Bible, Talmud, and codes to contemporary economics and sophisticated financial reporting—are worth the price of admission." —Rabbi Irving "Yitz" Greenberg

Why Israel (and its Future) Matters: Letters of a Liberal Rabbi to the Next Generation by Rabbi John Rosove. Presented in the form of a series of letters to his children, Rabbi Rosove makes the case for Israel — and for liberal American Jewish engagement with the Jewish state. "A must-read!" —Isaac Herzog, President of Israel
"This thoughtful and passionate book reminds us that commitment to Israel and to social justice are essential components of a healthy Jewish identity."
—Yossi Klein Halevi, author, *Letters to My Palestinian Neighbor*

Other Covenants: Alternate Histories of the Jewish People by Rabbi Andrea D. Lobel & Mark Shainblum. In *Other Covenants*, you'll meet Israeli astronauts trying to save a doomed space shuttle, a Jewish community's faith challenged by the unstoppable return of their own undead, a Jewish science fiction writer in a world of Zeppelins and magic, an adult Anne Frank, an entire genre of Jewish martial arts movies, a Nazi dystopia where Judaism refuses to die, and many more. Nominated for two Sidewise Awards for Alternate History.

Recent books from *Ben Yehuda Press*

Burning Psalms: Confronting Adonai after Auschwitz by Menachem Rosensaft. "It's amazing that Menachem Z. Rosensaft's *Burning Psalms: Confronting Adonai after Auschwitz* doesn't burst into flames. This book of poetry—every poem in it a response or counterpoint to every one of the psalms in the biblical book—written by the son of Holocaust survivors and the brother of a murdered sibling he never knew, is composed with fire, fueled by a combination of rage, love, and despite-it-all faith that sears your eyes as you read it." —*New Jersey Jewish Standard*

Blessed Are You, Wondrous Universe: A Siddur for Seekers. Non-theistic Jewish prayers by Herbert J. Levine. "Herb Levine has fashioned a sparkling collection of prayers for a thinking, feeling modern person who wants to express gratitude for the wonder of existence." —Daniel Matt, author, *The Essential Kabbalah*.
"An exercise in holy audacity." —Dr. Shaul Magid, author, *The Necessity of Exile*

Siddur HaKohanot: A Hebrew Priestess Prayerbook by Jill Hammer and Taya Shere. Creative and traditional Jewish rituals and prayers that explore an earth-honoring, feminine-honoring spirituality with deep roots in Jewish tradition. "Far more than a prayerbook, this is a paradigm-shifting guidebook that radically expands our religious language, empowering us to reclaim what our souls have known for centuries: how to cook, season, and feast on our love of life, Spirit, and each other." —Rabbi Tirzah Firestone, author, *The Receiving: Reclaiming Jewish Women's Wisdom*

Mussar in Recovery: A Jewish Spiritual Path to Serenity & Joy by Hannah L. with Rabbi Harvey Winokur. "A process of recovery that is physically healing, morally redemptive, and spiritually transformative." —Rabbi Rami Shapiro, author, *Recovery: The Twelve Steps as Spiritual Practice*.
"A lucid and practical guidebook to recovery." —Dr. Alan Morinis, author, *Everyday Holiness: The Jewish Spiritual Path of Mussar*.

Judaism Unbound (Bound): Provocative Conversations About the Jewish Future with the Most Visionary Thinkers and Practitioners by Dan Libenson and Lex Rofeberg, editors. "Those concerned about Judaism's future will find plenty to chew on in these creative and expansive dialogues." —*Publishers Weekly*

As the Story Goes: Funny, Strange, and Serious Stories of Yiddishland's Jews by Mordekhai Lipson; Jonathan Boyarin and Jonah Sampson Boyarin, translators and editors. A treasure trove of anecdotes that illuminate the lives, humor, and wisdom of Eastern European Jewish communities from the 18th and 19th centuries. A bestseller nearly a century ago in its original Yiddish, these stories capture the essence of a world where tradition and ingenuity intertwined.

The Secrets of Creation by Rabbi Meir Ibn Gabbai: Insights from Mysticism, Modern Science, and Art by Arthur Green, Debra Brand, and Howard A. Smith. Drawing from the 16th-century kabbalistic text 'Avodat ha-Kodesh by Rabbi Meir Ibn Gabbai, the book is a collaborative effort by a historian of Jewish mysticism, an astrophysicist, and a Hebrew manuscript artist. Together, they examine a kabbalistic narrative of Creation, weaving it with contemporary scientific insights and visual artistry to offer a multidimensional perspective on the origins of existence. "These three modern masters demonstrate how ancient wisdom can stimulate and enlighten us today. Delve into this book and you will be amazed!" —Daniel Matt, author of *God and the Big Bang*

www.ingramcontent.com/pod-product-compliance
Lightning Source LLC
Chambersburg PA
CBHW020201090426
42734CB00008B/906